Rethinking Holy Land

Rethinking Holy Land

A Study in Salvation Geography

Marlin Jeschke

 **Herald Press**

Scottdale, Pennsylvania
Waterloo, Ontario

Library of Congress Cataloging-in-Publication Data

Jeschke, Marlin.
  Rethinking Holy Land : a study in salvation geography / Marlin
Jeschke.
    p. cm.
  Includes bibliographical references and index.
  ISBN 0-8361-9317-2 (pbk. : alk. paper)
  1. Land tenure—Biblical teaching. 2. Land tenure—Religious
aspects—Christianity. 3. Palestine in the Bible. 4. Bible—Geography.
5. Bible—Criticism, interpretation, etc. I. Title.
  BS680.L25J47 2005
  263'.042—dc22
                                                        2005025458

RETHINKING HOLY LAND
Copyright © 2005 by Herald Press, Scottdale, Pa. 15683
  Published simultaneously in Canada by Herald Press,
  Waterloo, Ont. N2L 6H7. All rights reserved
Library of Congress Catalog Card Number: 2005025458
International Standard Book Number: 0-8361-9317-2
Printed in the United States of America
Book design by Sandra Johnson
Cover by Cathleen Benberg, A Distant Wind

12 11 10 09 08 07 06 05   10 9 8 7 6 5 4 3 2 1

To order or request information, please call
1-800-759-4447 (individuals); 1-800-245-7894 (trade).
Web site: www.heraldpress.com

To Elizabeth Jeschke

Contents

Foreword

A MAN ENTERED a New England estate, set up camp under the spreading trees on the sweeping lawn, lit a campfire, began preparing his evening meal.

"Get off my land. This is private property. You are trespassing," the owner said as he arrived home in his Jaguar.

"This wide lawn is unused, I am staking a claim," the man replied.

"This land belongs to me. You have no right to claim any part of it."

"How did you get it?"

"I inherited it from my father."

"Where did he get it?"

"He inherited it from his father."

"And where did he get it?"

"He fought the Indians for it."

"Then I'll fight you for it."

For millennia, the "I'll fight you for it" tradition of ownership by conquest and violent seizure has been the common assumption of how territory is gained, kept, then subdivided by the occupying citizens. It is the ground of the nation-state. Possession of property, especially of land, was created as a basic human defense—surveyors, stakes in the ground, plats of land, deeds of property, escrow, purchase, taking possession, lock and key, no trespassing.

What if all this stands on an erroneous assumption? What if the basic paradigm of how to possess land on which our nations stand is morally questionable and patently unjust and indefensibly false? What moral foundations can justify land seized, its inhabitants unjustly displaced or brutally destroyed?

In a shrinking world with an expanding population, land is the issue—owning, sustaining, caringly conserving, ecologically protecting, and wisely using this land. Who owns will define who lives. Who has land, and the right to gain its nurturance will survive. This essential fact shapes all that follows—borders, border crossing, migration, immigration, refugees, illegal aliens, food production, you and your children's and grandchildren's safety and survival.

Some things seem beyond challenge and outside the possibilities of change. Yet the rediscovery of a radically different way of viewing things can change the most elemental understandings of who, what, where we are and how we shall live. This round earth, since time immemorial known to be flat, circles the sun, from primal times known to rise and set, and swings among the stars, since the first clear night known as celestial lights. The illnesses we face, age old products of distempers, a preponderance of bad bile, temperature changes, witchcraft and evil eye, are the result of bacterial fellow travelers, viral invaders. The listing of primal unquestionable absolute assumptions that have been challenged and changed is longer than we know.

Constructive change comes either by going back to the foundation, finding another rock to build upon, or going into the future and finding a jointly shared, mutually necessary goal where all are needed if the object is to be gained. The first is the radical solution—to find another root (a radical) and draw on its power. The second is a visionary solution, to see what can be and press to obtain it.

Marlin Jeschke does us a radical service. He gets to the roots of our philosophy of property by addressing it with a theology of possessing land.

A radical book (a book that examines roots) unearths the foundational ideas that support our beliefs (explores the root ideas that validate our constitutions, convictions and assumptions) and identifies the tap roots that sustain us (the root ideas on which we act and by which we live). This is what Jeschke does in writing a theology of possessing land; he digs into the primal earth on which we stand and asks how we came to possess it. Did we receive it as gift, or take it as booty?

Two contrasting streams of theology flow through the Hebrew and Christian scriptures. The one, from Abraham through Jeremiah, Jesus and Paul sees land as a gift from God. The other from Joshua through the conquest, the monarchy, the myriad wars of land seizure and boundary disputes, to Constantine and state religion ending in nationalism as we know it. It results in a worship of land and flag that sees the territory of the nation-state as holy, sanctified by the blood of its heroes who died on the boundaries, defending or extending its borders.

Jeschke teases out these tangled and confusing theological tap roots, and like Jesus, his primary mentor, asks what does the promise that the humble, the meek, shall inherit (receive as gift) the earth mean? In doing so, he draws from those theologians of the Hebrew and Christian Scriptures who have explored the concept of land. But Jeschke makes his own unique contribution. He follows the root to the trunk where we all live on our own piece of property, in our safe community, and asks what possession means to us. He goes on out the branches to raise the questions of vision. Where are we going to turn as our needs multiply exponentially for this good earth?

Obviously, the struggle for possession of the place called "the holy land" is a central paradigm for any theology of land, or for any discussion of salvation geography. Jeschke has been involved with key theological thinkers and peacemaking strategists for five decades. He is thoroughly versed in its complexities and contradictions, its long and confusing history.

In an old cartoon, an Israeli says: "This land is ours. We took it from the Palestinians, who took it from the Ottomans, who took it from the Arabians, who took it from the Romans, who took it from the Greeks, who took it from the Persians, who took it from the Chaldeans, who took it from us. Of course, we took it from the Canaanites, who took it from the Shittites, who took it from the Hittites, who took it from the Perezites, who took it from somebody before them." The histories of human need for a home as well as lust for land run long, run deep, run fast.

This book offers no quick fix for the Israel/Palestine problems or any other locale's. It is not a program for intervention in crisis situations. It is a strategy for prevention through rethinking the basic assumptions that serve as justifications for the leaps of faith taken in committing ourselves to support and protect what is ours against all others, and sometimes far more just human claims. He recognizes that change takes generations and insists that it is each generation's task to generate constructive alternatives to those that have been less than just.

So Jeschke seeks to reexamine the causes of the insoluble dilemmas of contested territory and design strategies that lead to prevention of making the same wrong turns generation after generation. He even has the courage to suggest that we possess with a lighter touch, inspired by a love for justice that is greater than our lust for land.

His key belief is beyond dispute. The irenic way to possess territory is the only one that has ultimately worked. Those who receive the land as gift, with their theological roots firmly planted in peaceful, mutually negotiated, justly pursued, hospitably owned practices have heard the promise of God to Abraham.

In a wonderful story told late in the book, Jeschke makes a fascinating rejoinder to a student. He says, "My grandfather was born in Poland, my father in the Ukraine, my mother in South Dakota, I in Saskatchewan, my children in Indiana. I am part of a refugee and pilgrim people of God in the earth so that wherever we live, we are at home with God."

Far from being rootless, he speaks from an experience and a tradition rooted first in faith and second in soil. That order is significant. As one reads *Rethinking Holy Land*, one's most basic beliefs and future priorities get reordered.

> *David Augsburger*
> *Fuller Seminary,*
> *Pasadena, California*

Preface

THE FIRST INSPIRATION for this book came in the form of the late Frank Epp's *Whose Land is Palestine?* (1970). That succinct historical review prompted my first thoughts of a complementary theological assessment of the Israeli/ Palestinian conflict. Perhaps because of that interest I was invited to participate in a 1970s working group on that subject sponsored by Mennonite Central Committee (MCC) of Akron, Pennsylvania. That working group included also (at that time) Waldemar Janzen, Professor of Old Testament at Canadian Mennonite Bible College, Winnipeg, Canada; William Keeney, Professor of Religion and Peace Studies at Bluffton (Ohio) College; Elmer Martens, Professor of Old Testament at Mennonite Brethren Biblical Seminary, Fresno, California; and John K. Stoner, staff member at MCC. Since then Janzen and Martens have written on this subject, and their contributions are recognized in the bibliography. My ideas on this subject started taking shape in meetings of that working committee, though they have broadened to engage the general theology of possessing land.

I am grateful also to Goshen and Bluffton colleges for naming me the C. Henry Smith Peace Lecturer for 1978-79, which offered me another chance to work on this subject. And I am grateful too for other modest Goshen College faculty research grants, which helped me to attend an institute on Judaism at Vanderbilt University and spend several weeks reading at Hebrew Union College in Cincinnati and at Jewish Theological Seminary in New York. Despite bulging and growing files of notes, however, I was not able to produce a serious manuscript during my years of a heavy teaching load at Goshen College. The opportunity to write came after my retirement, when my wife and I were privileged to spend September through December of 1996 at Tantur, the Ecumenical Center for Theological Study in Jerusalem. We will always remember with gratitude Tantur's hospitality and witness on that hill-top beside the road between Jerusalem and Bethlehem. The first rough draft of this manuscript got scratched out in Tantur's quiet library.

My thanks also to a number of readers who looked at a penultimate draft of this manuscript: John Lapp, my former dean and provost at Goshen College and then Executive Secretary of MCC; John Fisher, former Goshen College faculty colleague; William Klassen, New Testament scholar; John W. Miller, Old Testament scholar; Ted Grimsrud, theologian and professor at Eastern Mennonite University; Michael King, editor at Cascadia Press; and Ervin Beck, also former Goshen College faculty colleague. Special thanks go to Levi Miller, director of Herald Press, Scottdale, Pennsylvania, and editor Michael Degan. I appreciate any and all suggestions they have offered, although heeding some of these suggestions would have meant a different book. I received help also from Steve Nolt and Paul Keim, professors at Goshen College, and from John E. Toews, former Dean of Mennonite Brethren Biblical Seminary, and recently retired from the Presidency of Conrad Grebel College in Waterloo, Ontario. My apologies in advance if I have overlooked anyone else who should have been named here.

I am indebted also to my son David, who set me up with convenient voice recognition software to let me compensate for my lack of keyboard skills and gave me other professional computer help. A special thanks to my wife Elizabeth, who was willing to surrender the final year of a public-school teaching contract at Chestnut Ridge in East Holmes County, Ohio, to accompany me to Tantur, and who has supported me in this project. I dedicate this book to her.

A problem with almost any book is the question of when to wrap it up. One could always postpone finishing a manuscript in order to add a footnote from another recent book or periodical, but one must finally bring writing to an end. The biblical tradition that I have sought to review still remains the last word for me on how we Christians should assess the subject of possessing land.

Marlin Jeschke
October 2005

Introduction:
Salvation Geography

THE YEAR 2007 will mark the 60th anniversary of the establishment of the state of Israel. From the point of view of most Israelis—and of many Jews around the world—1947 marked a momentous new era of freedom, power, and pride for Jewish people after centuries of exile, dispersion, persecution, wandering, discrimination, pogroms, ghettos, and above all the Holocaust. A few Jews in fact spoke hopefully of their restoration to the land as possibly the beginning of the "redemption," the messianic age.

Christian apocalyptists would like to see Israel's return to the land as the trigger for an eschatological countdown, the prerequisite to the unfolding of their dispensationalist scenario for the second coming of Christ. For the Hal Lindseys of America, the establishment of the state of Israel now invites the appearance of Antichrist, the rapture, the tribulation, Armageddon, and the realization of a thousand-year reign of Christ.

From the point of view of many Palestinians, however, the establishment of the state of Israel has meant invasion, displacement, refugee status, loss of property, occupation, oppression, torture, and for a good number death—an experience, in fact, like that of many Jews during many periods of their history.

Of course, other nations have also appeared or reappeared in many other parts of the world since the end of World War II in 1945. This new political geography may have brought them independence, but often also conflict, oppression, violence, and displacement. Yet something about the events swirling around the birth of modern Israel stirs Christian imagination in an extraordinary way, even if we concede that in the eyes of God every human life is of equal importance and worth, whether African, Asian, European, or American. Even if they don't see it freighted with apocalyptic significance, many Christians find the appearance of the modern state of Israel of special interest because the story of ancient Israel figures so prominently in the Old Testament, the root of every Christian's faith.

Of the many voices addressing the Middle East problem too many offer uncritical support for Israel, for whatever reason: guilt feelings about the Holocaust, alleged fulfillment of prophecy, or the view of Israel as God's chosen people. These voices characterize Palestinians as obstructionists to the peace process at best, terrorists intending genocide of Israel at worst.

On the other hand, too many other voices offer unqualified condemnation of Israel for its unethical expropriation of Palestinian land, displacement of Palestinian people, and occupation of Palestinian territory. These voices characterize Israelis as obstructionists to the peace process at best, guilty of their own kind terrorism and even war crimes at worst.

Of the voices that seek balance and mediation, too many engage in prodigious labor to try to broker one square inch of territory per change of government in either Washington or Jerusalem, but without changing lenses about the only real solution to the problem. Most proposals hitch peace and security to military power, never stopping to think that this land, once promised as a gift to Abraham and his descendants, was to be a model of a new way to possess territory and in that quite specific respect to be a light to the nations. The people who were promised this land have never to this hour been released or excused from that responsibility or task.

Nor, for that matter, have we. This book is actually not addressed to either Israelis or Palestinians but primarily to North American Christians. It is an invitation to Christians to see the Middle East dispute over territory in a new way, to discover the biblical paradigm of how to possess land. It is an invitation to examine salvation geography.

Land in the Bible

Land is an important theme in the Bible. And yet, says Elmer Martens, a "little research will show that theological discussion about land is almost totally absent in the literature until recently. This scarcity of exposition is surprising because 'land' is the fourth most frequent noun or substantive in the Old Testament: it occurs 2,504 times. Statistically land is a more dominant theme than covenant" (Martens, 103-4). There is no entry for "Land" in the first edition of *The Interpreter's Dictionary of the Bible*. But there is an excellent article by Waldemar Janzen on "Land" in *The Anchor Bible Dictionary*. Janzen echoes the observation of Martens, "The land theme is so ubiquitous [in the Hebrew Scriptures] that it may have greater claim to be the central motif in the Old Testament than any other, including 'covenant'" (146).

As we might expect, the subject of the land is not overlooked in Jewish scholarship. There is an article on it in *Encyclopedia Judaica*, but that article gives little attention to a theology of land. It is gratifying to mention a few of several books that have recently begun to focus attention upon this important theme: W. D. Davies, *The Gospel and the Land: Early Christianity and Jewish Territorial Doctrine* (1974, 1994); Walter Brueggemann, *The Land: Place as Gift, Promise, and Challenge in Biblical Faith* (1977, 2002); Norman C. Habel, *The Land Is Mine: Six Biblical Land Ideologies* (1995); and Philip Johnson and Peter Walker, editors, *The Land of Promise: Biblical, Theological, and Contemporary Perspectives* (2000).

We have all become acquainted with the term "salvation history," the story of God's salvation disclosed and wrought through the ages from Abraham to Jesus and until today. The term was made popular by Oscar Cullmann's *Christ and Time* (1951). This salvation we celebrate according to a religious calendar from Advent through Christmas to Easter and Pentecost. Much Christian writing, preaching, and teaching reviews this salvation history—how the purposes of God move forward toward their realization in the "fullness of time." By now salvation history has become a common locution in biblical theology and even in lay Bible study.

Salvation history, however, occurs in space as well as in time. Indeed, we speak of events "taking place." We are creatures of geography as well as of history. Every event of our experience of salvation, past and present, inescapably carries a geographical as well as a historical dimension. In the Jewish tradition this truth is obvious. And for Christians the Christ event permanently establishes Bethlehem, Nazareth, Capernaum, and Jerusalem as holy places because of where special events in the life and mission of Jesus took place. These holy places Christians recognize in pilgrimage, sometimes visiting Bethlehem at Christmas or the Church of the Holy Sepulcher at Easter, correlating their recognition of salvation history and salvation geography.

The recognition of salvation history is not, however, merely observance of the church year from Advent to Pentecost, when some churches make sure to get the right liturgical colors for the successive seasons onto altar or pulpit. The intent of salvation history is to perpetuate itself in a community that lives salvation, that fills its days and years with the new quality of life of the kingdom of God, thereby writing new chapters of salvation history. Similarly, the recognition of salvation geography is not merely an identification of holy places, erecting shrines there and making pilgrimage to them. Salvation geography means a community living out the distinctive style of possession of territory that salvation history teaches, receiving land as a gift from God and stewarding it with respect for neighbors and descendants, extending the reach of holy land. Salvation is not just our liturgical or even personal pietistic acknowledgment of God's actions at certain times and places, but also our sanctification of the time and space in which we live.

By salvation geography, therefore, I mean more than reverence for holy places and more than conscientious attention to those back-of-the-Bible maps of the holy land at various cross sections of salvation history. Or even those modern maps of the Middle East: Palestine after the 1948 cease-fire and Israel after the 1967 Six-Day War. These geographical studies merely put the question more acutely before us: what does it mean to receive the promise of land, to inherit it, to possess it, to be exiled from it, to return to it, to steward it, above all to sanctify it?

Conquest of Land?

Much of human history and even some of the Bible story assume that we acquire and maintain territory by force and violence, conquest and military defense. From ancient Egypt, Assyria, and Babylon through European colonists seizing land from Native American "Indians" to Saddam Hussein trying to get territory from Iran or Kuwait, people have sought to seize turf by conquest and bloodshed. Our libraries bulge with the narratives of territorial conquest in every age and on every continent and island on earth. That is why a major theme of the Bible, if we could recognize it, is salvation geography, God's attempt to bring salvation to bear upon the geographical dimension of human existence. Salvation history intends to teach us salvation geography. Salvation geography proposes to show us an alternative to fallen humanity's way of acquiring and possessing territory by violence and conquest.

Any review of the subject of salvation geography within the framework of salvation history must begin with several broad preliminary truths. Basic to all of them is the truth that God desires all human creatures to possess a home where they can dwell in security and peace. To that end God first provided a home in Eden, a garden that stands as a symbol for God's provision of a place where the human family can live in such security and peace. Eden also, unfortunately, becomes a symbol of failure to live in accordance with God's design, a reminder of exile and dispossession as a consequence of disobedience. But when humanity forfeited God's primal purpose, God's redemptive grace went to work: God called Abraham and Sarah and promised them and their descendants a home. T. Desmond Alexander draws attention to a hint that "the promised land was viewed as being, in part at least, a re-creation of Eden" (Johnson and Walker, 41). "The Jordan valley was well watered everywhere like the garden of the Lord" (Gen 13:10 RSV).

But God also assigned a territorial home to the Gentile

nations of earth, seventy of them according to traditional Jewish thought. The assignment of Canaan to Israel is seen as part of God's "primordial ordering of all lands," that is, granting all peoples a home (Habel, 41). According to the biblical story, nations persistently violated this divinely intended territorial order, and God then judged these nations with a view to eventually achieving a geographical order on earth that would reflect God's desire for all nations to coexist in mutual respect and peace. The description of the peaceable kingdom in Isaiah 11 is not often enough recognized as a geopolitical description of an ultimate state of affairs among nations in which the Assyrian lion, Babylonian ox, and Persian bear no longer prey upon the lamb of Judah—or upon each other—but rather accept God's territorial design, God's salvation geography. ("Design" is the felicitous term Elmer A. Martens uses in his *God's Design: A Focus on Old Testament Theology.*)

(We should note that in the Bible, and throughout much of human history a nation was an ethnic or linguistic group that usually possessed a self-conscious identity but often did not have clearly defined boundaries. Contrast this with the modern nation-state that often has a pluralist ethnic and linguistic population within clearly defined borders.)

A New Way to Possess Land

The thesis of this book is that from at least the time of Abraham to the present hour God has been trying to coach humanity toward a new way of possessing territory other than the way of seizing it by conquest and then defending it by violence and force. The promise of a land to Abraham and his descendants does not imply that God is not concerned about a territorial home for other peoples of the earth, or even that only a limited corner of the globe can be holy land. God intends the promise to Abraham to be a paradigm and the beginning of a process that results in the sanctification of the whole earth. Salvation history discloses a consistent purpose from the call of Abraham to the beatitude of Jesus that the meek shall inherit the earth to Paul's statement that God promised Abraham's descendants the world (Rom 4:13).

Possessing territory—a home—means more, we should note, than merely a deed or title to a lot and house, or acreage for industry or agriculture. It includes the broader natural landscapes of God's creation: lakes and streams, woods and meadows, mountains and deserts—and also cities and social infrastructures, cultures and the traditions that enrich our lives. In the case of Israel, this love of a particular spot on earth is totally obvious. Similar feelings are, however, shared by other people as well: Tanzanian fishermen on the shores of Lake Victoria, Swiss farmers in the valleys of the Alps, Canadians in the shadow of the Rocky Mountains, or Japanese hikers on Mount Fuji. They all have a God-given right to love their homeland, to see it as God's gift and to seek to dwell there. And they all have a responsibility to sanctify their God-given space.

Moreover, it is also the privilege and right of peoples besides Israel to identify places of pilgrimage that mark special events in their salvation history or that undergird their faith. Catholics have a right to make the Vatican a place of devotion and pilgrimage, as many of them do. Lutherans have a right to revere Wittenberg. Methodists have a right to treasure Aldersgate in London as the historic site of John Wesley's religious experience, marking the birthplace of Methodism. Kimbanguists of the Democratic Republic of the Congo have a right to cherish Kamba, their "New Jerusalem," as the place of God's visitation to them through the prophet Simon Kimbangu.

Too often, though, holy places become the occasion of unholy conflict. Witness the Church of the Holy Sepulcher in Jerusalem, and the Temple Mount. Holy places should prompt holy life—sanctified politics, economics, and international relations. Isaiah 2 and Micah 4 envisage Jerusalem as a place of pilgrimage and education for the nations. They see Jerusalem teaching the world the law of God, which would bring peace. So does Jesus in the triumphal entry into Jerusalem and in his "cleansing" of the temple. "My house," he says, quoting Isaiah 56:7, "shall be called a house of prayer for all the nations" (Mark 11:15-19). Some of the earliest Zionists such as Achad Ha'am hoped the Jewish return to Israel in the twentieth century would establish a kind of United Nations think tank to help solve many of the world's ethical problems. They were profoundly disappointed when this hope miscarried.[1]

This book is written for Christians who still take biblical faith seriously and are therefore willing to take a second look at what the Bible has to say about how we acquire and possess land, territory, space, turf. Modern theological and ethical writing addresses many issues of personal and social ethics: the implications of salvation for sexual morals, for business and industry, for ecology, for family, for education, for medicine, even for recreation and athletics. Too little attention has been devoted to what the Bible teaches on the big geopolitical question of possessing territory. This study will therefore focus upon a biblical theology of possessing land.

Our approach will be to reflect upon the story of ancient and modern Israel/Judaism with special reference to the subject of land. The Bible teaches salvation geography, from which we can draw some conclusions about how to regard the Middle East problem in a new way. But we decline to stop there. We Christians must find the biblical way of learning to sanctify land wherever *we* live in order to make it holy land. It would be easy to make moral judgments about both biblical and modern Israel/Palestine and allow that to deflect attention from equally serious problems at other times and places in the past and present, many of them closer to home. That is why we must review what the Bible has to say about salvation geography.

— 1 —
Abraham:
The Promise of Land

The LORD said to Abraham . . ., "Raise your eyes now, and look from the place where you are, northward and southward and eastward and westward; for all the land that you see I will give you and your offspring forever. I will make your offspring like the dust of the earth; so that if one can count the dust of the earth, your offspring also can be counted. Rise up and walk through the length and breadth of the land, for I will give it to you" (Gen 13:14).[2]

THE PROMISE OF THE LAND to Abraham and his descendants has long been recognized as one of the most basic givens in Israelite and Christian faith. God did not promise Abraham a new sexual ethic or better health or a new morality in family life or a superior culture or even that his descendants would be among the top violinists of the world. These were all potential blessings, but realizable only if Abraham and his descendants possessed some space on earth where their faith and its fruit could flourish. Culture, the sciences, the arts and civilized life cannot blossom and flourish among people who are perpetually homeless. The promise to Abraham therefore addressed the most basic problem of the human race, the problem of finding a home by overcoming greed, violence, and conflict in the possession of territory.

On that reading we may note the connection between the promise of the land and the promise that Abraham's descendants would be a blessing to all families or nations of the earth. These two are inextricably connected. It is especially by modeling how to possess land and how to sanctify it that Abraham and his descendants were to bless the world. The promise of the land to Abraham and to his descendants and the checkered account of its fulfillment are important for our subject not only because of the promise of the land itself, but also because of *how* Abraham, Isaac, and Jacob came into possession of that land and because of how they lived in it.

Abraham as a Model

For centuries Jewish rabbinic thought considered Abraham a model of Jewish faith and obedience, much as Christians have regarded the apostolic church depicted in the Acts of the Apostles as a model of faith and obedience. Genesis 26:5 says (God speaking to Isaac), "Abraham obeyed my voice and kept my charge, my commandments, my statutes and my laws." Talmudic reflection upon this text claimed that Abraham must have observed the injunctions of Torah given much later under Moses, even though living centuries before the time of Moses: "In haggadic literature Abraham is regarded as having observed all the commandments, . . . even though they had not yet been revealed. He acted in strict conformity with the Oral Law: 'No one occupied himself so much with the divine commandments as did Abraham'" (*Encyclopedia Judaica*). We are not told whether Abraham kept these ordinances out of intuition or by virtue of personal divine guidance. It is fitting, then, to look into the ethical practice of Israel's founders with respect to the land.

(1) The first point we must note in God's promise of the land is that it was a gift, as Walter Brueggemann emphasizes in his seminal book, *The Land* (1977, 2002): "The land to Israel is a gift. It is a gift from Yahweh and binds Israel in new ways to the giver. Israel was clear that it did not take the land either by power or stratagem, but because Yahweh had spoken a word and had acted to keep his word" (47). According to Elmer Martens, "There are eighteen explicit references in Deuteronomy to the Lord's promise of land to the patriarchs, and all but three speak of God's giving it" (Martens, 108).

Readers of the Bible have too generally missed the significance of the land as a gift. To receive land as a gift stands in striking contrast to the way territory was usually acquired in Abraham's time and too often throughout human history—armed conquest.

Abraham's acceptance of the land as a gift is therefore decidedly not incidental to the narrative of Israel's origins. It represents a divinely-intended break with the all-too-common method of acquiring space, and in that respect it signifies the very first objective of the salvation history that begins with Abraham. In other words, and it bears repeating: when God calls Abraham and Sarah, the very first and most important characteristic of redeemed existence, marking its break with fallen humanity's pattern of life, is this new way of coming into possession of territory—to receive it as a gift of God and to possess it peacefully. All other commandments given subsequently to the founders and their descendants about circumcision, sacrifices, Sabbath observance, feasts, the tabernacle and the temple are secondary to receiving the land as a gift. All other commandments actually presuppose and are dependent upon having some God-given place to observe them—and the requisite peace to be able to do so. As Abraham and Sarah represent the beginning of salvation history, so also do they represent the beginning of salvation geography. The very first purpose of salvation history is to inaugurate salvation geography. Salvation history and salvation geography are corollaries.

Coexistence with Neighbors

(2) The second point to note about the patriarchs/matriarchs is their willingness to coexist with other inhabitants of the land. In his book *The Land Is Mine: Six Biblical Land Ideologies* (1995) Norman Habel says, "It is my contention that the Abraham narratives reflect a distinctive immigrant ideology that views the land as a host country and its inhabitants as potentially friendly peoples. The . . . ideology in these charter narratives, I would argue, is in conflict with most of the [other] ideologies" of the Old Testament. The Abraham narrative "depicts Abraham as an immigrant. . . . The land seems open to migrants. . . . Canaan is depicted as a peaceful place to live, a welcome host country for immigrants and settlers. . . . The land is not empty, but neither is it hostile. . . . Abraham . . . identifies himself to the Hittites as a *ger* [sojourner] residing in their midst (Gen 23:4). . . . The nation of Abraham's seed is supposed to empower, not disempower, other nations of the host country. . . . The territory to be possessed is identified in terms of its ten indigenous inhabitants: the Kenites, the Kenizzites, the Kadmonites, the Hittites, the Perizzites, the Rephaim, the Amorites, the Canaanites, the Girgashites, and the Jebusites (Gen 15:19-21). This classic list might conjure up memories of the conquest tradition, but no explicit indications are given here that these people are to be expelled or destroyed. On the contrary, the narratives

that surround this land covenant suggest that Abraham provided a model of how to live at peace with the host peoples of the land and share ownership of the land. In this ideology, possessing the land does not demand annihilation or expulsion of these peoples" (Habel, 115-25).

To note the pertinent high points in the stories of Abraham, we see that he shared the land with his nephew Lot, even magnanimously granting Lot the watered Jordan Valley and himself accepting the territory around Beer Sheba and Hebron (Gen 13:5-12). Abraham also paid respect to Melchizedek, King and priest of Jerusalem (Gen 14:18-20). And finally, upon the death of Sarah, Abraham bought a burial plot from the Hittites, the cave of Machpelah. Ephron the Hittite offered him both "the field . . . and the cave that is in it," but there must have been some good reason why Abraham insisted on buying it (Gen 23:11). Would acceptance of the field and cave as a gift have made Abraham a feudal vassal? In any case, the purchase of the plot was in keeping with the policy of fair and amicable coexistence with other inhabitants of the land and not inconsistent with receiving the land as God's gift.

The story of Isaac and Rebecca repeats the fundamental theme of the Abraham/Sarah narrative. Like Abraham, Isaac lived in peace with other inhabitants of the land. When the herders of Gerar contended twice with Isaac's servants over wells dug by his servants, Isaac yielded and dug a third well, saying, "Now the LORD has made room for us, and we shall be fruitful in the land" (Gen 26:22).

When we come to the story of Jacob, the immediate ancestor of the people Israel, we notice at the outset a fateful twist in his experience of acquiring the birthright from his brother Esau, a birthright that included the promise of the land. The moment Jacob got the birthright he had to leave the land. Fleeing to Haran in Mesopotamia to escape

Esau's murderous anger, he labored for his uncle Laban in exile from the land he had just inherited. Jacob is to be commended, however, both for his appreciation of the Abrahamic heritage, and for his perseverance and patience in remembering the land and returning to it rather than remaining in Haran.

But mark the conditions under which Jacob was able to return. When he did return after an absence of twenty years he had to first come to terms with his brother Esau. It is a moving scene of fraternal reconciliation. Jacob had the advantage of the birthright. Esau had the advantage of actual occupation of the land. Jacob was profoundly deferential. He said, "Accept my present from my hand; for truly to see your face is like seeing the face of God—since you have received me with such favor" (Gen 33:10). In turn Esau was magnanimous in forgiving Jacob for how he had finagled the birthright. The result of their meeting was coexistence in the land (Gen 32:3–33:17).

One cannot help interjecting a word about the powerful parable the story makes of what should have happened and should be happening in the modern history of the Middle East in the return of Jacob's descendants and their encounter with the descendants of Esau. Would that the descendants of Esau had received the descendants of Jacob with favor! Would that the descendants of Jacob too might have seen in Esau's descendants the face of God!

Sojourning with God

(3) A third point to note about the founders of Israel's faith is the sojourning character of their life in the land. The Abraham and Isaac clans both temporarily left the land because of famine and then returned. Jacob absented himself for twenty years before returning. Possession of the land did not therefore exclude temporary emigration. The

founders discovered enough security in the promise of God to be able to leave and return. They truly were sojourners.

The question may be raised whether the Abraham, Isaac, and Jacob clans really possessed the land. Several texts seem to imply that the promise of possession applied not to the patriarchs themselves but only to their descendants. "To your offspring I will give this land," says Genesis 12:7, and "To your descendants I give this land" (Gen 15:18), although Genesis 15:7 says, "I am the LORD who brought you from Ur of the Chaldees, to give *you* this land to possess" (emphasis added), and Genesis 17:8 says, "And I will give to *you, and to your offspring* after you, the land where you are now an alien, all the land of Canaan" (emphasis added). Nevertheless, a widespread view would have it that although the patriarchal/matriarchal clans were *promised* the land, that promise did not get fulfilled until the conquest under Joshua and perhaps not fully until the kingship of David. He was the one, it is popularly held, who vanquished Israel's enemy neighbors, especially the Philistines, and finally established secure borders as conditions for Israel's true possession of the land.

There is one obvious sense in which the patriarchal clans did not possess the land. Being only a family or clan, even with many servants, Abraham's household was patently not big enough to occupy all of the square miles of even the small area from Dan to Beer Sheba between the Mediterranean and the Jordan.

In also another sense Abraham did not really fully possess the land, nor for that matter did Joshua. Or even King David. And even today Israel does not yet truly or fully possess the land—and will not even after the completion of the security barrier. Full and secure possession is not possible for any one people apart from neighbors who also renounce conquest, respect territorial integrity, and thus also sanctify their land. Abraham may have been a model of coexistence with his neighbors, but some of those neighbors were not. Abraham's nephew Lot was the victim of a plundering raid by an army of Chedorlaomer (Gen 14:11-16). Abraham organized the 318 men of his household as a "posse" to rescue Lot and his family and retrieve the loot. However, the rescue of Lot, whatever violence it involved or did not involve (the Bible does not give us any body count), was clearly not over the acquisition of land.

No one can have perfect, final, and secure possession of land until all people on earth accept the biblical vision of salvation geography and cease the practice of trying to grab someone else's territory. In every chapter of history possession of the land of Canaan—and of any land—has therefore been proximate, imperfect, in process. To claim complete possession pretends a control of the narrative of salvation history before it is fulfilled. Perfect possession is an eschatological ideal that awaits a future full realization of the kingdom of God. Present life under the rule of God is imperfect and incomplete for us in many respects. And yet it is our privilege to possess land on the example of Abraham today.

To question whether Abraham really inherited the land is tantamount to questioning whether he really inherited salvation. In historic biblical thought, as Paul says in his letter to the Romans, Abraham is considered the primal recipient of salvation, and the most basic blessing of salvation he and his clan received, as already noted, was the redeemed mode of geographical existence. Abraham was granted the opportunity of dwelling within the land freely. Indeed, he was invited to walk to and fro in it. Moses later did not get the privilege of entering the land; he saw it only from afar. Abraham, however, entered it and is buried there. He was a sojourner with God in the land, the divinely ordained way of true possession (Gen 23:4).

Later texts, represented as coming from the time when Moses was instructing Israel in the course of its way from Egypt to the promised land, inform Israel that its people would always be sojourners in the land. Being sojourners is part of salvation geography, the way of possessing land God is trying to teach humankind. A candid reading of the biblical narrative shows Abraham, Isaac, and Jacob and their families to be living as securely with God in the land as the later Hebrew tribes and Israelite kingdoms did—to be living in more promising security, if anything, than the people of the subsequent nation-state.

The picture in the biblical record may be the opposite of our modern biases. It is Israel's founders who model faithful possession, the more secure sojourning with God in the land, whereas the rise of the monarchy and nation-state signal the beginning of the slide into exile and expulsion from the land. Our notions of normative possession of the holy land too often reflect modern Western (and unredeemed) notions of possession of territory, notions colored by capitalist and even colonialist possession, as for example the American pioneers' seizure of American Indian land. Or the dispossession of homeowners for a new mall in suburban America. These are notions that need to be revised in the light of the biblical model of salvation geography.

No Boundaries

(4) A fourth and perhaps most important point in the promise of the land to Abraham deserves mention here. He was invited to walk to and fro in the land to survey it. God's promise is broad: "All this land will I give you." We are not told how far Abraham walked or how much he saw (though it likely was not as hazy at that time as it so

often is today). The point is, God did not define any boundaries or limits to what Abraham was to receive. It was left completely open.

The boundaries are much discussed in both biblical study and today's debates over the contemporary Middle East problem. The most common boundaries mentioned are Dan to Beer Sheba and, of course, the Mediterranean to the Jordan, plus perhaps the land of Bashan, loosely identified today as the Golan. Some Old Testament references include all the territory from the Brook of Egypt to the Euphrates, including much of what is today Syria and southern Lebanon. The "empire" of David is claimed to have embraced this larger area. But numerous scholars and commentators agree that for most of its history Israel basically populated and controlled only the area west of the Jordan from Dan to Beer Sheba.

The absence of a mention of boundaries in the promise to Abraham may well have a momentous geographical import, only hinted or suggested by implication. God promised Abraham that his descendants would be as many as the stars of heaven (Gen 15:5-7). And Jacob was promised that his offspring would be like the dust of the earth (Gen 28:14). In Genesis 32:12 Jacob invokes the promise of "offspring as the sand of the sea, which cannot be counted because of their number." These promises seem to expect a greater number of faithful and obedient descendants than the territory from Dan to Beer Sheba could ever possibly hold. Are we shortsighted in assuming, as most readers of the Bible seem to have assumed, that the promise embraced only the territory from Dan to Beer Sheba, with a Hebrew-Israelite-Jewish population restricted to this limited area? Must we in fact assume a fixed and static boundary at all?

Suppose Abraham and Sarah's descendants had lived

in faith and obedience and grown to 300 million, or might yet do so. Such a population could not be confined to the area from Dan to Beer Sheba. Many devout descendants of Abraham and Sarah would need to live as far away as Turkey, Greece, Egypt, or even Iraq (or New York or Chicago or Miami?). And yet they could surely cherish Hebron and Jerusalem as much as inhabitants of Tel Aviv or the Golan do today. Theirs would not be a case of living outside the land but rather a case of revisioning the scope of the land.

It seems to me more valid to read the promise as envisioning a growing population of devout people of the covenant who cherish the holy centers of their faith but whose growth requires moving, growing "boundaries," or new definitions of boundaries, or perhaps no boundaries at all. And the expectation of growing boundaries could hardly require the continuous and indefinite displacement of previous inhabitants embraced within those growing boundaries, certainly if those inhabitants adopted Abrahamic faith. Indefinitely moving boundaries would spell coexistence with the people already living in areas encompassed by those growing boundaries and enable the fulfillment of the promise that through Abraham and his descendants all the families of the earth would be blessed. Indefinitely growing boundaries—or actually, the elimination of boundaries—would mean the unhindered spread of God's people and of the new way of possessing land.

The fulfillment of the promise that Abraham would be a blessing to the nations is stifled when limited to a tiny geographical area, though even according to the vision of Isaiah and Micah other nations coming up to the mountain of the house of the LORD would do so in order to learn his ways, including above all to learn God's new way of appropriating and stewarding space. It is lack of faith and vision to expect that the covenant people would forever remain the few million that can be crammed into that corner of Asia from Dan to Beer Sheba. To be sure, God's promise to Abraham never intended to lose the later identification of the holy centers that emerged—Hebron, Bethlehem, Jerusalem, and for us Christians also Nazareth and Galilee—but God's promise to Abraham was intended to be the beginning of a process through which the whole earth would eventually become holy land.

My reading of the promise to Abraham is not arbitrary in the light of what we will see in the mission of Jesus and in Paul's word in Romans 4:13 that Abraham's descendants "would inherit the world [cosmos]." Whatever the original meaning of Psalm 37, the text Jesus quotes in Matthew 5:5 about the meek inheriting the land/earth, Jesus and Paul interpret for us what God was trying to tell Abraham—namely, that the promise had as its obvious design the salvation and sanctification of the whole earth. In that sense the promise to Abraham in Genesis 13:14 already spells out God's intention for salvation geography. The promise of the land to Abraham pointed to a new way of possessing territory around the world. It is to the subsequent fortunes and misfortunes of that vision to which we now turn.

— 2 —
Hebrews: Exodus and Conquest

THE BIBLE follows the narratives of Israel's founders with the account of Israel's sojourn in Egypt, the exodus, wilderness wandering, and then conquest and settlement in the land. The books of Exodus to Deuteronomy, a fairly extensive block of literature, deal repeatedly with the subject of the land, even before Israel set foot in it. According to the broad consensus of biblical scholarship, this block of literature as it now stands was written, or at least compiled and edited, at a later period of Israel's history, perhaps during the time of King Josiah, hundreds of years after Israel's entrance into the land, and it is selective, reflecting later ideas of what transpired or should have transpired on the way to the land and during its conquest and settlement.[3]

Before we turn to an assessment of this literature we raise, parenthetically, a question not often pondered. Why did the descendants of Jacob settle down in Egypt for the 430 years that Exodus 12:40-41 says they did and not return to the land soon after the famine in Canaan was over? Surely the famine back in the land of Canaan did not last that long. Did Israel put comfort and security in Egypt ahead of appreciation of the land? The sojourn in Egypt certainly contrasts with later expressions of love for the land (Ps 137, for example). And Israel's failure to seek an early return to the land compares unfavorably with the records of Abraham and Isaac after famines (Gen 26:1) and of Jacob's timely return. Surely the Hebrews in Egypt were not hindered from returning soon after coming to Egypt, as they were much later after a new Pharaoh subjected them to slavery.

Some biblical texts claim the Hebrews were delayed in their entrance into the land because the cup of iniquity of the prior inhabitants was not yet full (Gen 15:16). This invites the suggestion that if Jacob's descendants had returned earlier and not waited for 430 years, their life and witness in the land might have prevented the degeneration of Canaanite society—or might even have converted many Canaanites to Hebrew faith. The 430-year delay of the Hebrews in returning to the land had so increased their number that it precipitated the convulsions of the "conquest."

Whatever our answers to the foregoing questions, one thing is clear: Israel's exodus from Egypt became a biblical paradigm for God's deliverance, as liberation theology emphasizes. But Egyptian slavery also became a symbol of what any society should not be or do—suppress minority populations or aliens and subject them to slavery. Egypt became a byword for oppression and injustice. Having been "brought up from Egypt" emerged as a formula refrain in Israel's scriptures to remind them of deliverance from an unjust social order. And yet, as we will see, Israel perpetrated these injustices against minorities in the promised land once they got there.

The books of Exodus through Deuteronomy have much to say to the Hebrew tribes on their way from Egypt to the promised land about life in that land to which they were headed.

God's Land

(1) Israel was repeatedly reminded that God was the owner of the land and that they were therefore only sojourners with him. "The land shall not be sold in perpetuity, for the land is mine; for you are strangers and sojourners with me" (Lev 25:23 RSV). They were never to sell the land because it was not theirs to sell. Further, they were not free to do with or in the land what they wished but were obligated to live according to the commandments and directions God prescribed. Again, as sojourners themselves, they were to offer humane treatment to the stranger and sojourner among them, not forgetting how they were treated in Egypt. "Israel's status with Yahweh was similar to that of an alien with an Israelite" (Martens, 111).

Gary M. Burge points out that the law "of ancient Israel made generous allowances for 'the alien (or sojourner)'. . . . Aliens were accorded surprising privileges. . . . They were included in religious ceremony and worship . . . [and] were to have access to the same system of justice enjoyed by the Israelites" (Burge, 80-81).[4]

(2) God gave Israel an extended list of commandments to observe in the land (Exod 21-23), of which the "ten words" of the Decalogue (Exod 20) were only the beginning. God enjoined them to avoid the idolatry and abominations of the Canaanites. God prescribed laws for agriculture, for family and sexual life, for arbitration of grievances, and for festivals and liturgical life. In brief, God called them to be a righteous people, a "holy nation" (Exod 19:6, a phrase repeated in 1 Pet 2:9).

God repeatedly warned the people that possession of the land was conditional. If they did not observe the commandments prescribed, if they lapsed into unrighteousness, then the land would become polluted and would vomit them out the way it vomited out its prior inhabitants. "But you shall keep my statutes and my ordinances and do none of these abominations . . . lest the land vomit you out, when you defile it, as it vomited out the nation that was before you" (Lev 18:26-28 RSV).

"The land becomes the touchstone for life or death; it is given out of God's free grace, but retained by means of obedience" (Janzen, 147). Disobedience might necessitate deportation, exile, though not revocation of the promise. These were the sentiments echoed in Jeremiah when he condemned the kingdom of Judah for its sins, predicted exile, and counseled acceptance of exile. However, even if God took Israel into exile, the people had a right to seek to return to the land to dwell once more as sojourners with God, but again to receive the land as a gift and to dwell in it strictly under the conditions laid down by their covenant God.

Atrocities of the Conquest

(3) In addition to the themes just mentioned there appears another shocking one quite inconsistent with the two just discussed. According to Deuteronomy in particular, God instructed Israel in how to deal ruthlessly with the inhabitants of Canaan, and the book of Joshua shows to what extent these instructions were executed. Some of these texts describe what God would do, going before Israel in holy war, while other texts have God commanding Israel to do it. Several of these texts deserve citation here. To adapt a word of caution occasionally given on TV, readers are warned that this material is graphic, and reader discretion is advised![5]

> •Israel was told, "When the LORD your God brings you into the land that you are about to enter and

occupy, and he clears away many nations before you . . . and when the LORD your God gives them over to you and you defeat them, then you must utterly destroy them. Make no covenant with them and show them no mercy" (Deut 7:1-2).

- Israel was told it must "dispossess and destroy" the prior inhabitants of the land, a command that is given twice (Deut 9:1-5, and 12:29-30).
- Israel was told it would inherit "great and goodly cities, which you did not build, and houses full of all good things, which you did not fill, and cisterns hewn out, which you did not hew, and vineyards and olive trees, which you did not plant" (Deut 6:10-11 RSV).
- The people were told, "You must not let anything that breathes remain alive. You shall annihilate them—the Hittites and the Amorites, the Canaanites and the Perizzites, the Hivites, and the Jebusites—just as the LORD your God has commanded" (Deut 20:16-18).

I have cited only the more gruesome texts here. We could also note Deuteronomy 20:10-14, which prescribes "forced labor" even for inhabitants of Canaanite towns that accepted Israel's terms of peace. Where towns resisted, all males were to be "put to the sword. You may, however, take as your booty the women, the children, livestock and everything else in the town." This permission of plunder does not accord with other texts that prescribe "cherem"—that is, the consecration of property to God in destruction so that Israel would not, it was hoped, engage in war for the sake of plunder (see the story of the fall of Jericho, Joshua 6:17-7:21, where Achan is stoned for violating this rule of holy war, and 1 Samuel 15:1-35, where the prophet Samuel faults king Saul for not obeying the rules of holy war).

In the Book of Joshua we read how the instructions of Deuteronomy were carried out.

- Jericho was consigned to oblivion: "Then they devoted to destruction by the edge of the sword all in the city, both men and women, young and old, oxen, sheep, and donkeys" (Josh 6:21).
- At Ai Israel massacred 12,000 people: "And Israel struck them down until no one was left who survived or escaped. . . . The total of those who fell that day, both men and women, was twelve thousand—all the people of Ai. For Joshua did not draw back his hand, with which he stretched out the sword, until he had utterly destroyed all the inhabitants of Ai" (Josh 8:22, 25-26).
- At Makkedah, Joshua "utterly destroyed every person in it; he left no one remaining" (Josh 10:28).
- In "the whole land" Joshua "left no one remaining, but utterly destroyed all that breathed, as the LORD God of Israel commanded" (Josh 10:40).
- At Hazor "they put to the sword all who were in it, utterly destroying them; there was no one left who breathed" (Josh 11:11).
- Joshua 11:14 repeats the refrain, "All the spoil of these towns, and the livestock, the Israelites took for their booty; but all the people they struck down with the edge of the sword, until they had destroyed them, and they did not leave any who breathed."
- In other parts of the country Joshua "put them to death" (Josh 11:17). People were "exterminated" (v. 20), "utterly destroyed" (v. 21).

Israel thus engaged in four different and related kinds of action in what is commonly called the conquest of the land: (1) dispossession or expropriation of land and confiscation of property on it, (2) subjugation and enslavement of some inhabitants, (3) expulsion of others, and (4) extermination or slaughter or annihilation of still others. In Deuteronomy and Joshua these actions are reported with no question about their morality.

These texts have, however, raised questions in the minds of scholars for both historical and theological-ethical reasons. Perhaps they have not raised enough questions in the minds of lay readers, because the policies here prescribed and described must be judged sub-human. Their modern labels are plunder, slavery, ethnic cleansing, and genocide—crimes against humanity condemned on all sides today by civilized and humane people, crimes for which perpetrators are brought before international tribunals.

Assessing "Holy War"

We acknowledge that the Jewish community as a whole has long since risen above this kind of conduct. Already the Wisdom of Solomon (12:8-10) rationalizes that God destroyed the Canaanites "little by little; though [God] was not unable . . . to destroy them at one blow . . . but judging them little by little [God] gave them an opportunity to repent," of which the Canaanites apparently did not avail themselves (Charles, 1:554). The Haggadic commentary on Leviticus says Joshua sent messengers beforehand, offering the Canaanites the options to leave, to make peace, or to fight, and their fate was decided by their choice.[6] "To avoid the embarrassment that the Jews had not dwelt in the land from time immemorial and had occupied the land of the Canaanites, some writers went so far as to claim that the land was uninhabited before the arrival of the Jews" (Wilken 1992, 32).

According to David Flusser, rabbinic literature is not happy with Old Testament descriptions of the conquest and its atrocities. Medieval rabbis spoke practically nothing about Joshua. Rabbinic literature did stress the promise of the land, but separated it from the subject of war. For most Jews of the Middle Ages war was disagreeable, and they did not think of war as an implication of the promise of the land.[7] John Howard Yoder claims that in the exile most Jews became a "peace church" and that the "pacifist" Jesus is therefore not an anomaly but true to his heritage (Yoder 2003, 69-87). "Rabbi David Hartman, an Orthodox rabbi and philosopher living in Israel today, suggests how he reads the book of Joshua, 'I'm here to correct the mistakes of Joshua. I don't want to live with Joshua as a permanent model of how Jews build the land'" (Quoted in Brenneman, 103).

And yet some radical Zionists today are tempted by this strand in their biblical tradition, as we saw at Deir Yassin in the war of 1948 and some of the events in the Six-Day War of 1967, and still see today in the expropriation of land from Palestinians.

Also today most people in the Christian community would claim that Christ leads us above this level of behavior, though people who call themselves Christians have, in the name of God, engaged in Joshua-like ethnic cleansings and genocides. Witness the Crusaders in their capture of Jerusalem in 1099, the American treatment of Indians, above all the Holocaust in Nazi Germany, most recently the Hutu massacres of Tutsis in Burundi and Rwanda (most Hutus were Catholic Christians), and the conduct of Serbs in Bosnia and Kosovo. As we have seen in recent times, modern society seeks to bring persons guilty of such atrocities or war crimes to trial before international tribunals.

Because this is part of canonical literature, Christians must take some thought about how to deal with it, to put this account into perspective. They must offer some quite specific guidelines on how to counter its dehumanizing influence.

(1) In modern times some Christians have simply spiritualized—and evaded—these texts in a fashion akin to medieval allegory. The commands of holy war in Deuteronomy and Joshua are said to stand for our fight against sin and our destruction of the "flesh." Some interpreters intuitively read these texts as we do the story of Hansel and Gretel (which also contains a grisly scene) and relegate these stories in Joshua to some imaginary world, some never-never land not located on this planet. But, as Michael Prior shows in *The Bible and Colonialism: A Moral Critique*, the Joshua texts surface periodically to fuel and to justify crimes against humanity, as they did in the European conquest of the Americas and in the Boer settlement of South Africa.

(2) Devout popular interpretation would claim the severity of ancient Israel's policy is occasioned and justified by the religious practices of the Canaanites. Deuteronomy 7:5 says, "But this is how you must deal with them: break down their altars, smash their pillars, hew down their sacred poles, and burn down their idols with fire. For you are a people holy to the LORD your God." As one writer puts it, because of practices such as child sacrifice and cult prostitution, "their culture had reached the depths of pagan depravity" (Burge, 74). If Israel thought its destructive actions were indeed divinely sanctioned, that policy is prohibited with the advent of Christ, whose gospel recognizes no people as beyond the reach of salvation, regard-

less of how depraved. Mission annals of the past 200 or 300 years are full of stories of the Christianization of societies just as depraved as those of ancient Canaan. The conventional view of Israel's destruction of Canaanites forgets that God had salvation purposes for these people too.

Pleading divine support for one's cause because of the wickedness of an enemy is too often a rationalization for war crimes. Justifying genocide by appeal to divine sanction looks less credible to its victims, especially when it is God's people who are the victims. No matter how many of today's American preachers popularly decry America's moral degeneracy, most of those who voice these condemnations would be the first to call for military defense against any force that God might send today or tomorrow to exterminate some or all of wicked America for its sins.

(3) Another interpretation of these texts suggests that Joshua represents a later simplified and glorified and even exaggerated account of what occurred. Some writers go so far as to suggest that the book of Deuteronomy originated, or at least reached its present form, during the time of Josiah or even when the returning Jewish exiles encountered the Samaritans and wrote what they thought their forebears *should* have done upon initial entrance into the land (Prior, 227). Internal evidence of this is a text such as Deuteronomy 30:3-5, "The Lord will *restore* your fortunes . . . gathering you *again* . . . And the Lord your God will bring you into the land *that your ancestors possessed.*" These verses indicate that the text as it now stands looks back from a time possibly as late as the exile. As Walter Brueggemann says, "The final form of the text is completely removed from what may have been the 'happening' of land, and now function as a belated ideological rationale for the subsequent community of Israel."[8] As another interpreter explains it, the book of Joshua may report only

a successful series of battles of the Hebrews against a coalition of three Kings (Josh 9:1-2. Anderson, 131-42). If so, the book of Joshua describes only part of the larger process of Israelite entrance into the land, ignoring extensive peaceful infiltration and settlement, and focusing instead upon the sensational, as do today's newspaper, radio, and television reporters.

The book of Judges shows that Israel never killed or drove out all the Canaanites of the land. In fact, Israel was unable to do so, as the first chapter of Judges candidly admits. And therefore the Hebrew tribes lived in relatively peaceful coexistence with many Canaanites most of the time, eventually even intermarrying and assimilating culturally. They made a covenant with the Gibeonites (Josh 9:3-27) even though, according to texts such as Exodus 23:32 and Deuteronomy 7:2, they were not to make any covenants with the previous inhabitants. The Hebrews even went to war as allies of the Gibeonites on one occasion. It is the story of the sun standing still until Joshua finished the battle (Josha 10:6-14).

Any reflection requires us to note the inconsistency between biblical injunctions to treat the alien and sojourner with kindness and justice and the instructions to exterminate the prior inhabitants of the land. Extermination would leave no alien or sojourner to be treated with kindness and justice!

On the whole, Old Testament scholars conclude that much of Israel's occupation of the land was a relatively peaceful—or at least nonviolent—infiltration and settlement. A recent view, in fact, holds that much of the Hebrew tribal confederacy came into existence in the land as a result of the revolt of a coalescence of dissident people together with the Hebrews, people disadvantaged in the political and economic development of the times (Gottwald).

These considerations soften the overall picture but still do not excuse those atrocities Israel did commit, even if one were to plead that enemies of the Hebrews engaged in the same kind of conduct, which may be true enough. Israel was called to be a different kind of people.

Choosing a Land Ideology

(4) A more appealing and reasonable—and biblical—way to deal with the stories of the atrocities of the conquest is to read the canon with discrimination. As already mentioned, Norman Habel claims there are several distinct and different land ideologies in the Hebrew Scriptures, some of them quite inconsistent with each other. He is surely right, because some later prophets of Israel evidenced a very different point of view and spirit than that shown in Deuteronomy and Joshua, thanks no doubt to the experience of Israel on the receiving end of war atrocities at the hands of numerous enemies, chiefly the Assyrians and Babylonians, though also of smaller neighboring peoples such as the Edomites, Ammonites, Moabites, and Syrians.

Prophets such as Isaiah project a picture not of extermination but of salvation and coexistence with the nations of the earth (the peaceable kingdom of Isaiah 11). Ezekiel, speaking of Israel's restoration after the exile and the reallocation of the land, says, "You shall allot it as an inheritance for yourselves and for the aliens who reside among you and have begotten children among you. They shall be to you as citizens of Israel; with you they shall be allotted an inheritance among the tribes of Israel. In whatever tribe aliens reside, there you shall assign them their inheritance, says the LORD God" (Ezek 47:22, 23). Later Jewish thought proposed that wicked nations might not be destroyed but turned to God and brought to salvation, as the book of Jonah shows. Certainly those following Christ and taking seriously the great commission of Matthew 28:18-20 and Acts 1:8 would insist that that is God's way.

There may be some Jews in modern Israel, and even fanatic Christians in the Western world, who find justification in Deuteronomy and Joshua for what Israel today in diplomatic language calls "population transfer." For them the modern "conquest," continuing with annexations, is a justifiable rerun of at least some aspects of the story of Joshua.

Concluding Observations

(1) We must make a distinction between the exodus and the conquest. We are justified in celebrating the liberation of the Hebrews from Egyptian slavery, but we are not required to endorse the violence perpetrated in the conquest. Those acquainted with the story from Sunday school days may be accustomed to accepting it as one whole. As one Native American remarked, "As long as people believe in the Yahweh of deliverance, the world will not be safe from Yahweh the conqueror" (quoted in Prior, 282).

There is a serious inconsistency between the exodus and the conquest. The exodus celebrates the deliverance of a subject people from enslavement and extermination. How can a sensitive reader of that narrative countenance the enslavement and extermination of another subject people by those just delivered from it? Victor Frankl, a survivor of a Nazi concentration camp, speaks of the risk of a brutalized people developing a tendency to do to others what was done to them.[9] Maybe that is why there are numerous texts warning Israel to remember how they were treated in Egypt.

(2) The history of Israel tells us that something went

wrong during the time of the monarchy, so seriously wrong that it eventuated in the fall of the nation and the deportation of many Israelites to Assyria and Babylon. Such is the claim of the prophets. A candid reading of the biblical narrative persuades us that something went wrong earlier, already during the time of the Hebrew tribal confederacy. Wars of conquest represented a gamble that required raising the ante. The violent conquest had already set the Hebrew tribes on the path of making enemies. The alternatives were either to retreat from that pattern, or to raise the stakes by going all the way to nation-statehood—and accepting the consequence: exile. Israel's policies were, as Jeremiah warned, political suicide.

(3) Whatever our inclination in interpreting these troubling texts of Deuteronomy and Joshua about the conquest, Christians must finally make a choice among the several land ideologies in the Old Testament, for some are incompatible with others. I don't know if I would find six, as Norman Habel does. But certainly the view of the land found in the patriarchal narratives and in prophets such as Jeremiah, culminating in Jesus and Paul, is so different from that found in the conquest and monarchy that we must make a choice.

The choice that much of Constantinian Christianity made privileges the conquest and monarchy ideologies, and reads the patriarchal narratives and even Jesus through those lenses. In the thinking of most Christians Israel did not really possess the land until the time of Joshua or David. For them Jeremiah's counsel to accept exile, and Jesus's word that the meek shall inherit the earth, merely represent a hiatus, an interim, until Armageddon will once again resort to violence to settle the question of possession of the land. On this interpretation readers seek biblical blessing for the ideology of worldly conquest instead of patiently reading the whole biblical narrative to find which way God is trying to lead the human race in possession of land, the way truly, fully, and finally disclosed in Jesus Christ and the apostolic Church.

Wars of territorial conquest with their attendant atrocities are not compatible with the message of Jesus. And Jesus, as we will see, while seeking to make Jerusalem the center of worldwide salvation and of a universal community of faith, repudiated violence and revolt to recover an independent Jewish state. The repudiation of violence has fortunately been shown also in the ideal of the Christian world mission, if not often enough in its record. The commitment of the church has been to evangelize people, no matter how depraved—head-hunting savages and "idol worshippers" and moral reprobates on the streets of America who surely are no less degenerate than even the most iniquitous Canaanites ever were.

(4) We must not, however, conclude with the critique of Israel found in our rereading of the story of the exodus and the conquest, sobering and salutary as that is. If the subject is the extermination of peoples, who is guilty of the greatest act of genocide in known history? Christians, if we can call them that, have killed more Jews over the centuries in pogroms and the Holocaust than ancient Israel ever killed in the conquest under Joshua and Judges and in the history of the modern state of Israel. When we Christians look at the Crusades, European treatment of North American natives, the massacres in Rwanda and Burundi, and the genocide of Bosnians, the relevant observation is that too many Christians have not risen above the conduct of the Hebrews at the time of Joshua (for a fuller account see James Carroll, *Constantine's Sword: The Church and the Jews*, 2001). Christian crimes of conquest and killing cannot be excused by pleas of separation of

church and state, as though these crimes were perpetrated by the state, not the church, when these two were so often combined in a state church, or just as effectively combined in an uncritical patriotism and church endorsement of state violence.

— 3 —

Israel: Monarchy and Nation-State

BOTH 1 SAMUEL 8 AND DEUTERONOMY 17 see the transition from tribal confederacy to kingship in Israel to be freighted with far-reaching consequences. The monarchy had implications for the internal economic, political, and religious life of Israel and for Israel's foreign relations.

Israel's decision to move into the monarchy, a state with centralized power, was prompted by two concerns, internal and external. The internal, the need for law and order, shows up already in the admission of Judges 17:6 and 21:25, "In those days there was no king in Israel; all the people did what was right in their own eyes." The external, defense against outside enemies, is indicated in the repeated, insistent demand for a king reported in 1 Samuel 8:19, 20, "But the people refused to listen to the voice of Samuel; they said, 'No! but we are determined to have a king over us, so that we may be like other nations, and that our king may govern us and go out before us and fight our battles.'"

These then are the two concerns: "govern us" and "fight our battles." The monarchy, the centralized state, was supposed to be the answer to domestic anarchy and foreign threats. The demand for a king reflected the belief that in order to survive, Israel would need to meet on their terms the nation-states of the world among which they lived. It was a powerful temptation, and the consequences showed up in Israel's subsequent experience. The nation-state showed impressive success in the short run but incurred problems in the end that proved to be a high price to pay.

Deuteronomy 17:14-20, written as if with an eye on the career of Solomon, offers cautious permission for monarchy, provided Israel met certain basic conditions. It stipulates that Israel's king was to be one of their own, not a foreigner. Having said this, the text adds three prohibitions and one positive injunction. The king was not to multiply horses, specifically in trade with Egypt, a warning against militarization, for chariots were the military technology of the day. This injunction is already in tension with Israel's request for a king to fight the nation's battles. Further, the king was not to "acquire many wives," a large harem, a warning against domestic and foreign alliances cemented by marriages. Finally, the king was not to amass silver and gold. This was a warning against the kind of taxation or monopoly of trade that would eventuate in a class society, stratifying the population into a rich aristocracy oppressing the poor. The one positive injunction: the king was commanded to provide himself a copy of God's law, study it and rule the nation by it.

The 1 Samuel 8:4-22 story of the rise of the monarchy contains similar explicit warnings, but these are preceded by the forthright statement: "The LORD said to Samuel, 'Listen to the voice of the people in all that they say to you; for they have not rejected you, but they have rejected me from being king over them. Just as they have done to me, from the day I brought them out of Egypt to this day, forsaking me and serving other gods, so also they are doing to you.'" These words constitute a serious charge. Monarchy represented loss of faith in God in favor of trust in worldly powers. Then, at the behest of God, Samuel, like Deuteronomy 17, warned Israel of evils that the kingship would entail: (1) conscription of Israel's manpower for military service, (2) conscription of labor, (3) expropriation of land, (4) taxation of produce, and (5) enslavement of people (1 Sam 8:11-18). The Samuel account thus identifies the central issue: monarchy carried inevitable consequences for ill. Samuel tells the people, as John Howard Yoder puts it, "You'll be sorry" (Yoder 1997, 60). In their decision Israel was unfortunately copying the ungodly political pattern of the nations around it instead of providing a sanctified alternative political model for other nations to follow.

The biblical objection to monarchy in Israel should not be read as a rejection of human leadership or of administrative structure as such. The rule of God requires human leadership, and in their history Israel had leaders such as Moses and Samuel and Ezra. The alternative, as already noted, was that "everyone did what was right in his own eyes." The issue remained the nature, quality, and authority of human leadership, and its purpose. Prior to the rise of the monarchy, leadership was charismatic, not dynastic— that is, leaders were raised up by the spirit of God. That implied a leader who possessed the gift to inspire and truly lead, and leadership was to be for the good of the people and not for the king's self-aggrandizement. Above all, leadership was to create a just, peace-loving, and compassionate social order.

Israel's monarchy provided a quick fix for the problem of the Philistines, at least with the advent of David, but Israel ended up paying a rather steep price in the long run.

Implications of the Monarchy

The transition to monarchy entailed the creation of borders. No longer did Hebrew tribes live as a covenant community with a distinct religious identity among other peoples, and other peoples among them. Having become a boundaried state, Israel inherited many non-Hebrew subjects who were now to be assimilated into the nation, pagan remnants of the seven or ten nations of Canaan repeatedly mentioned in Joshua and Judges. These people were now to be absorbed as taxable subjects, potential conscripts for the military, or a labor pool for the state's (king's) building projects, especially fortifications. Solomon's census counted 153,600 "aliens," whom he subjected to forced labor (2 Chron 2:17). These non-Hebrew people constituted the perennial temptation of high places, pagan worship, and idolatry that seduced Israel. There were among them, to be sure, devout converts such as Uriah the Hittite, who observed the rules of holy war despite King David's ulterior designs. Many, however, instead of being assimilated, continued as an indigestible pagan element within what was supposed to be the Yahweh-worshipping state of Israel.[10]

With the advent of the monarchy and the creation of boundaries Yahwist faith became a state religion, one token of which was the attempt of kings to forcibly suppress local idolatrous shrines in order to center faith upon the temple in Jerusalem. A state religion incurs both internal and external problems, as we have seen in the history of state churches in Europe.

The internal problem is what to do with dissenters, nonconformists, and unbelievers—or God-sent prophetic critics—within the state. The common temptation is to use coercion, which can be harsh, as in Judah's destruction of "high places" and Solomon's drafting of aliens for public labor, treating non-adherents of the state religion as second-class citizens.

In this vein Israel sought periodically to suppress the practices of resident pagans through coercive measures, such as desecrating high places, cutting down Asherim, destroying altars to idols, and the like. We read of such measures taken by kings Asa (c. 913-873 B.C.E., 2 Chron 14:3), Hezekiah (c. 715-687/6, 2 Kings 18:4; 2 Chron 31:1), Jehoshaphat (c. 873-849, 2 Chron 17:6), and Josiah (c. 640-609, 2 Chron 34:6, 7). For example, under Hezekiah "all Israel who were present went out into the cities of Judah and broke down the pillars, hewed down the sacred poles, and pulled down the high places and the altars throughout all Judah and Benjamin, and in Ephraim and Manasseh, until they had destroyed them all." It didn't change hearts. Israel's faith may have proposed to be ethnic by virtue of descent from Abraham, but in fact, like Christian faith, it could ultimately be only voluntary, and a genuine faith could not be a state religion, pretending to embrace all inhabitants of a given national geographic area.

The monarchy produced other fateful consequences for Israel's internal life. Samuel's prediction that the king would enslave his subjects became all too true during the reign of Solomon, in the very second generation of the Davidic dynasty. We see Solomon doing to his own subjects what the Pharaoh had done to the Hebrews in Egypt, that in spite of many reminders in Israel's scriptures that God had brought them up out of Egyptian bondage. It was the forced labor during Solomon's reign that led to the revolt under Jeroboam, the secession of the ten Northern tribes, and the division of the one people Israel. Another example of the fulfillment of Samuel's prediction was Ahab and Jezebel's expropriation of Naboth's vineyard (1 Kings 21).

We should note that the classic prophetic movement arose with the advent of the monarchy. "It is because of kings that prophets appear" (Brueggemann, 91). The monarchy produced so many evils that God raised up a succession of prophet-critics to point out where Israel missed its calling. In prophets such as Amos, Hosea, Isaiah, and Jeremiah we read a litany of grievances: high-handed policies of the monarchy, the polarization of society into rich and poor, the subversion of justice in the courts by the wealthy and privileged, sexual immorality, drunkenness, and other indulgences that the luxury of the monarchic order invited—even alliances with pagan nations to shore up the regime.

According to prophetic indictments, Israel's sins added up to a desecration or pollution of the land, prompting fulfillment of the promise that under such conditions the land would vomit Israel out too, as it had some of the earlier inhabitants. In having a king to govern them and to fight their wars "like the nations," Israel patterned itself after the surrounding nations and adopted the social order of the surrounding society, which had been condemned for polluting the land. And so Israel again polluted the land. The irony is that, in Israel's request for a king in order to be like the nations, they became like those nations to the point of sharing their fate.

Wars of Conquest

State boundaries created by the transition to monarchy generated not only internal problems but external ones as well. In becoming a nation-state Israel joined the big leagues, the game of international politics. Here the first round, the defeat of the Philistines, may have looked like a resounding success. But King David did not seem to be satisfied with repulsing Philistines in wars of defense. He followed these with wars of aggression, conquest, and empire building, subjugating the nations of Edom, Moab, Ammon, and Aram (Syria) to Israel's rule and tribute. In a war with Moab, his great-grandmother's people, David made "them lie down on the ground [and] measured them off with a cord; he measured two lengths of cord for those who were to be put to death, and one length for those who were to be spared" (2 Sam 8:2. The account does not specify whether "them" refers to captured soldiers or males in general). According to 2 Samuel 8, in a war with the Arameans David's army killed 20,000 men and in a war with Edom 18,000. King David's war with the Ammonites may have been precipitated by a big misunderstanding over the intentions of Israel's peaceable embassy (2 Sam 10), but the Ammonite king Hanun's suspicions of that embassy may have had justifiable warrant in the light of David's conquest of Moab, Ammon's neighbor. After a defeat of the Ammonites David enslaved its population (2 Sam 12:31). In another war with the Arameans, he killed 40,000 (2 Sam 10:18). These conquests incurred enduring hatreds and bequeathed to David's heirs the burden of either perennial defensive wars against the understandable revolt of subject nations or, more often, the humiliation of defeat and shrinking borders.

Incidentally, what was the extent of "holy land" in this period of shifting boundaries in Israel's history? Did land switch from unholy to holy and back to unholy, depending upon whether it was "possessed" by the nation of Israel? The truth is, the whole land was desecrated by the wars themselves.

A sense of Israel's faith as a faith for all humankind, potentially at least, appears occasionally in the early history of the monarchy. In Solomon's eloquent oration at the dedication of the temple he includes this moving petition:

"Likewise when a foreigner, who is not of your people Israel, comes from a distant land because of your name—for they shall hear of your great name, your mighty hand, and your outstretched arm—when a foreigner comes and prays toward this house, then hear in heaven your dwelling place, and do according to all that the foreigner calls to you, so that all the peoples of the earth may know your name and fear you, as do your people Israel, and so that they may know that your name has been invoked on this house that I have built" (1 Kings 8:41-43).

And in Isaiah 2 and Micah 4 we find the prediction that "In days to come the mountain of the LORD's house shall be established as the highest of the mountains, and shall be raised up above the hills. Peoples shall stream to it, and many nations shall come and say: 'Come, let us go up to the mountain of the LORD, to the house of the God of Jacob; that he may teach us his ways and that we may walk in his paths.' For out of Zion shall go forth instruction, and the word of the LORD from Jerusalem. He shall judge between many peoples, and shall arbitrate between strong nations far away; they shall beat their swords into plowshares, and their spears into pruning hooks; nation shall not lift up sword against nation, neither shall they learn war anymore; but they shall all sit under their own vines and under their own fig trees, and no one shall make them afraid; for the mouth of the Lord of hosts has spoken" (Mic 4:1-4).

In the light of David's wars of conquest against his neighbors—Philistines, Edomites, Ammonites, Moabites, and Syrians—how many of them would be inclined to come up to the mountain of the house of the LORD to "beat swords into plowshares" to "learn war no more"? The state religion of a nation indulging in military aggression would not likely gain many converts among its enemies.[11]

State Religion

The boundaries of Israel as a nation-state therefore became also, unfortunately, boundaries to the faith. The vision of Israel during the period of the monarchy did not extend much beyond its borders. In this respect Israel's faith seemed to share the character of the territorial religion that governed the beliefs and practices of numerous peoples around Israel at the time—that is, the view that a specific god (or Baal?) ruled a given area, and that to live in that area required recognition and worship of that god, almost like fealty to a local feudal lord. It is illustrated in the story of Naaman the Syrian, the leper healed through Elisha (2 Kings 5). Naaman confessed faith in Israel's God, the God of all the earth. And yet he took back with him two mules' burden of earth when he returned home in order to be able to step onto Israelite turf when worshipping Israel's God back in Aram. If Israel's faith was the service of the God of all the earth, and its mission was to bless the world, the monarchy was surely not the way to go about structuring its geo-political life.

Toward the end of the monarchy, when increasing turbulence overtook the national life of Israel and Judah and they found themselves buffeted by conflict with surrounding nations, prophets such as Jeremiah began to see some of the implications of Israel's monotheism—that their God was indeed the God of all the earth and that this realization called for a new vision and new policies. Four aspects of this new vision were (1) that God was at work not only in Israel but also in other nations, using them for his universal purposes, perhaps to discipline Israel; (2) that Israel's faith could survive the collapse of the monarchy, the nation-state, and find itself unrestricted by the boundaries of Dan and Beer Sheba; (3) that God purposed salvation

for other peoples besides Israel, indeed the salvation of all
the earth; and (4) that both Israel's salvation and that of
other peoples was to be achieved by a new geo-political
arrangement other than a monarchic state.

We are obliged to conclude that on balance the venture
into kingship and the move into a conventional nation-
state form of existence did not really solve Israel's territorial
problems and bring them fulfillment of the promise of the
land to Abraham. It incurred a heavy penalty instead.
Monarchy became, to borrow a phrase from Brueggemann,
the "royal road to exile." Deuteronomy warned that
unrighteousness, failure to keep covenant, would lead to
the land vomiting out its inhabitants. Already when
Solomon had finished building the temple, God appeared
to him in a dream and warned, "If you turn aside from following me . . . and do not keep my commandments . . .
which I have set before you, but go and serve other gods
and worship them, then I will cut off Israel from the land
which I have given them; and the house which I have
consecrated for my name I will cast out of my sight; and
Israel will become a proverb and a byword among all peoples. And this house will become a heap of ruins" (1 Kings
9:6-8 RSV). According to 1 Kings 14:15 (RSV) the prophet
Ahijah sent word to Jeroboam, first king of the seceded ten
northern tribes, "The LORD will smite Israel . . . and root
up Israel out of this good land which he gave to their
fathers, and scatter them beyond the Euphrates, because
they have made their Asherim, provoking the LORD to
anger."

When the exile came, exilic and post-exilic writers one
after another reiterated this assessment. It became an
almost reflexively intoned formula: exile happened
because "Israel sinned against the LORD." What were the
sins? Pre-exilic prophets such as Amos and Micah, Isaiah

and Jeremiah, cataloged them: sexual immorality, alcohol abuse, economic exploitation of the poor, injustice in the courts, greed ("adding field to field"), moving boundary markers of property. The sins added up to Israel's failure to live out the ethics of salvation geography, and that sin, if not inherent in the nature of a monarchic state itself, was a direct consequence of Israel's choice to become a state "like the nations." Israel and Judah made enemies and violated their own integrity by acquiring land by violence and then trying to defend it by violence. It was the prescription for eventually and inevitably becoming the victims of violent invasion and conquest themselves, getting vomited out, deported, exiled.

To pose the issue of the monarchy in its most fundamental terms, when the Bible begins with the account of the creation of the whole human race before it gets to the call of Abraham, and when the stories of Abraham, Isaac, and Jacob mention five times that in Abraham and his descendants all families of the earth would be blessed (or "bless themselves"), is God's ultimate purpose in the call of Abraham a nation-state of some 7,847 square miles with a state religion? Or is God's intention a faith that will find its way into every part of the earth and bring salvation to anyone willing to embrace it? (The five references to the blessing of all families of the earth through Abraham are Genesis 12:3; 18:18; 22:18, speaking to Abraham; 26:4, speaking to Isaac; 28:14 speaking to Jacob; cited also in Acts 3:25 in the apostle Peter's speech, and in Galatians 3:8 by Paul).

Assessing the monarchy within the framework of the whole narrative of salvation history, we must conclude that it was not the way to realize salvation geography.

— 4 —
Judaism: Deportation and Dispersion

POPULAR READING of the Old Testament story, noting the sentiments of Psalm 137, usually sees the exile as tragedy and disaster, even if it is called a divinely ordained chastisement of Israel. "By the rivers of Babylon, there we sat down and wept, when we remembered Zion. . . . For there our captors asked us for songs, . . . saying, 'Sing us one of the songs of Zion!' How could we sing the LORD's song in a foreign land? If I forget you, O Jerusalem, let my right hand wither! Let my tongue cling to the roof of my mouth, if I do not remember you, if I do not set Jerusalem above my highest joy!"(vv. 1-6). The psalmist has no hesitation in voicing vengeful sentiments. "O daughter of Babylon, you devastator! Happy shall they be who pay you back for what you have done to us! Happy shall they be who take your little ones and dash them against the rock!" (vv. 8-9).

The prophets of Israel had a different take on the deportation. Already Amos ("For three transgressions of Judah/Israel, and for four, I will not revoke the punishment") and then with heightened seriousness the prophets Jeremiah and Ezekiel, living at the time of the exile and experiencing it, called the discipline of the exile inescapable and God's just measure for Judah's sins.

Jeremiah reported on those who refused to see the seriousness of the deportation. The prophet Hananiah blustered a prediction of a short exile. "Thus says the LORD of hosts, the God of Israel: I have broken the yoke of the king of Babylon. Within two years I will bring back to this place all the vessels of the LORD's house, which King Nebuchadnezzar of Babylon took away from this place and carried to Babylon. I will also bring back to this place King Jeconiah son of Jehoiakim of Judah, and all the exiles from Judah who went to Babylon, says the LORD, for I will break the yoke of the king of Babylon" (Jer 28:2-4).

Over against this unrealistic prediction Jeremiah offered his counsel. Writing to the exiles in Babylon he said, "Thus says the LORD of hosts, the God of Israel, to all the exiles whom I have sent into exile from Jerusalem to Babylon: Build houses and live in them; plant gardens and eat what they produce. Take wives and have sons and daughters; take wives for your sons, and give your daughters in marriage, that they may bear sons and daughters; multiply there, and do not decrease. But seek the welfare of the city where I have sent you into exile, and pray to the LORD on its behalf, for in its welfare you will find your welfare" (Jer 29:4-7). According to John Howard Yoder, "'Seek the peace of the city' is too weak a translation for Jeremiah's instruction. It should be translated, 'Seek the salvation of the culture to which God has sent you'" (Yoder 1997, 76).

We don't know how many exiles in Babylon actually received Jeremiah's counsel, but whether because of it or because of the Jews' resort to the inherent meaning of their faith, many Jewish exiles did what Jeremiah advised. On that reading, their heed to Jeremiah's counsel added up to nothing less than the sanctification of the new land in which they found themselves. The incongruity should not be lost on us: Jews were exiled because of their desecration of their own holy land but now engaged in the sanctification of unholy pagan Babylonian land. They now adopted the shape of life and community that they should have adopted earlier in their own land.

Seeking Nationalist Restoration

Jewish history following the exile actually showed two tendencies, one that followed the counsel of Jeremiah and one that hankered after a restoration of a Davidic kind of Jewish state. This latter desire persisted in the Jewish community for over seven centuries (and has, of course, reappeared today). Following the first return of exiles shortly after the edict of Cyrus, ca. 538 B.C.E., Haggai pinned his hopes, it appears, upon one Zerubbabel, a prince of the House of David, for a restoration of the kingdom. "Speak to Zerubbabel, governor of Judah, saying, I am about to shake the heavens and the earth, and to overthrow the throne of kingdoms; I am about to destroy the strength of the kingdoms of the nations, and overthrow the chariots and their riders; and the horses and their riders shall fall, every one by the sword of a comrade. On that day, says the LORD of hosts, I will take you, O Zerubbabel my servant, son of Shealtiel, says the LORD, and make you like a signet ring; for I have chosen you, says the LORD of hosts" (Hag 2: 21-23). Haggai's hopes were frustrated.

Attempts at a restored Jewish state flared up again, and more powerfully, in the Maccabean revolt of ca. 175 BCE and the short-lived Hasmonean kingdom, then in the insurrection in Jerusalem leading to the Jewish War of 66-70 C.E. and the ensuing siege of Masada, and finally in the abortive attempt of Jews in the land to achieve independence under Bar Kochba in 135 C.E.

Jewish attempts to restore an independent state came

from those who had returned to the land, and both popular and scholarly interest tends to focus upon them, maybe because of literature such as Josephus's *The Wars of the Jews*. Yet the majority of Jews lived outside the land from soon after the time of the deportation on, continuing to disperse (hence the term "the Diaspora," borrowed from the Greek). "The Jewish population in the Diaspora [at the time of Paul] was three times as large as in Palestine" (Toews, 23-24). And it was these Jews who followed the counsel of Jeremiah who really provided the intellectual leadership of world Judaism. For a millennium and more, Babylonian Jews shaped the development of classic Judaism, as shown by the emergence of the larger and more influential Babylonian Talmud and the recognition of Babylon rather than Jerusalem as the center of Diaspora Jewish religious authority. Alexandria too became a powerful and creative Jewish intellectual center.

On one reckoning Israel/Judah/Judaism should have disappeared with the destruction of Jerusalem and the deportation of its leading citizenry. Peoples such as the Philistines, Ammonites, and Moabites did disappear. The fact that the Jewish people and their faith survived, even flourished, shows that their identity was shaped by something much deeper and more permanent than the nation-state. In fact, the end of the nation-state and the deportation stripped away one identity to permit Israel to recover a truer identity and calling. What was that changed identity?

Finding a New Identity

For one thing, in the exile Israel seems to have been permanently cured of that idolatry which, according to the prophets, perennially plagued its people in the land, even after a centralized monarchy tried to restrict worship to Jerusalem. It seems to have been a constant battle for the

Jews to shut down the "high places" or shrines of pagan worship in the land. To cite the blunt language of the prophets, the people for some reason repeatedly went "a whoring" after other gods. But from the time of the deportation on, a faithful remnant took seriously the central tenet of Jewish faith, "Hear, O Israel, the LORD our God, the LORD is one." The stories in the first six chapters of the book of Daniel show the resolute anti-pagan, anti-idolatry convictions Jews developed in the Gentile world, such that Jews were willing to face death rather than compromise their worship of the one true God.

Furthermore, in the exile Israel's life no longer revolved around king and palace with its military establishment but around synagogue and Torah. In the land and under the monarchy as a nation-state, Jews were Jews by default. Now in the dispersion Jewish identity was not decided by geographical boundaries but by attendance at synagogue, study of Torah, and observance of the injunctions of Torah in personal life. Those not committed to Jewish faith were free at any time to disappear into the pagan Gentile world, and no doubt many did. Those committed to the life of Torah were required to signify that fact by deliberate, volitional identification with Jewish peoplehood. Jews were no longer Jews by default but by choice.

The exile also offered Israel a global vision it did not seem to have had before, as seen in Isaiah 40-55, for example, as well as in other prophets such as Jonah. Pushed beyond the horizons of the nation's borders, Israel increasingly emphasized the truth of God as God of all the earth and of all its people, a God concerned for all the world's salvation. With that Israel's prophets recognized the opportunity of a mission to the nations and the possibility of an eschatological age of peace among the nations. Living among Gentiles, Jews became a witness that led to the conversion of many Gentiles, the making of proselytes. We see something of the mature development of an outreach to Gentiles in the book of Acts. The apostle Paul's address in the church at Antioch of Pisidia reported in Acts 13:16-41 is directed to "you Israelites, and others who fear God," the latter referring to Gentile half-proselytes who related to the synagogue as what we today might call associate members.

As another feature of its new identity and strategy for survival, Judaism adopted what has often been called a concern for ethnic purity. Popular reading of Jewish history often sees this emerging concern as racial prejudice. It may in fact be seen as a concern for preservation of the faith, as we notice in the books of Ezra and Nehemiah, which report these leaders breaking up mixed marriages. They were concerned about marriages where children no longer knew Hebrew and therefore were in danger of being lost to the faith. The apostle Paul shares that concern when he counsels "marriage in the Lord" (1 Cor 7:39). For some other Jews, concern for marriage within the faith did not, however, require divorce. They accepted the more confident approach of proselytization. Why not bring Gentiles into the faith, as the book of Ruth proposes? We see this approach reflected in both Paul and Peter, who counsel believers in a mixed marriage to seek to remain in it with the hope of conversion of the unbelieving spouse (1 Cor 7:12-16; 1 Pet 3:1-2). Timothy was the product of a mixed marriage who remained with the faith.

Exile as Vocation

John Howard Yoder speaks of "exile (galuth) as vocation," the patient acceptance of Diaspora existence as God's assignment in the present age for both preservation of the Jewish community and salvation of the Gentile world. "According to Psalm 137, those first exiles asked, 'How can we sing the LORD's song in a foreign land?' Yet painful as the question is, that is what the Jews learned to do, and do well" (Yoder 1997, 56). The majority of Jews came to accept exile as normative Judaism and remained in exile even when they could have returned to the land.

Although it looked like a tragedy to those first exiles, the Diaspora turned out to be a blessing for both Judaism and the Gentile world. Jeremiah predicted an exile of seventy years to purify the land because of Israel's failure to observe jubilee for 490 years (2 Chron 36:21). But even Jeremiah's expectations fell short of God's intention. Israel's exile was not just a seventy-year hiatus before a return to its prior status, but God's invitation toward a new and more enduring mode of existence. What the exile achieved ended up being much wider—the sanctification of innumerable other places on the globe where Jewish goodwill contributed to the cultural and spiritual well-being of Gentile societies.

The choice of the majority of Jews to live in "exile" over the millennia has never, even today, erased a longing for the land, for home. Wherever Diaspora Jews celebrated the Passover celebrants would say, "Next year in Jerusalem," as an expression of an eschatological hope. Exilic and postexilic prophets did not drop the theme of restoration to the land, but a new motif appeared in connection with their promises and expectations of reentry after the deportations of 721 and 587 B.C.E. That motif was the salvation and transformation of Israel's neighbors, even its traditional foes. Where the original entrance under Joshua spoke the language of callous displacement of original inhabitants and basically ignores surrounding nations except to curse some of them because they impeded Israel's passage toward the land, the promised reentry exhibited a much more international consciousness. Israel had become inescapably aware of neighboring peoples, because the fortunes of its renewed existence in the land depended upon the goodwill of those neighbors. Therefore, according to prophets such as Second Isaiah, Israel's restoration was to be accompanied by and facilitated by the salvation of surrounding nations in order that they might be prepared to let Israel—and each other—live in peace. This, I think, is the import of the Isaiah 11 vision of the peaceable kingdom, the lion lying down with the lamb.

Toward the end of the letter to the Romans, Paul strings together a chain of Old Testament texts to document the Jewish expectation of a coming era of salvation of Gentiles. In Romans 15:9-12 he quotes from Psalm 18:49, Deuteronomy 32:43, Psalm 117:1, and Isaiah 11:10. To cite only the Psalm 117:1 text, "Praise the Lord, all you Gentiles, and let all the peoples praise him." In these citations Paul shows that the Jewish community was well aware of the hope of the salvation of the Gentiles articulated in their scriptures.

According to John Howard Yoder one modern Jewish scholar, Stephan Zweig, "sees the scattering of the Jews . . . not as a detour for only the next seventy years after 587 BCE, but as the beginning of the mission of the next millennium and a half. . . . The move to Babylon was not a two-generation parenthesis, after which the Davidic or Solomonic project was supposed to take up again where it had left off. It was rather the beginning, under a firm, fresh prophetic mandate, of a new phase of the Mosaic project" (or "Abrahamic project." Yoder, 1997, 53). The books of Ezra and Nehemiah may carry hints of a desire to return to a nation-state. However, we see the returned exiles being led by a scribe, Ezra, whose very title, scribe, authority in Torah, reflects a new role or office in postexilic Judaism. Although, according to Ezra 7:25-26, Artaxerxes gave Ezra broad discretionary powers for administration

of the returned exiles "whether for death or for banishment or for confiscation of goods or for imprisonment," in
the end neither Ezra nor Nehemiah is reported to have
resorted to any of those four measures, but to have leaned
upon instruction in Torah. In this pattern of life of
Diaspora Judaism we see the blueprint of the Christian
church, a people called into being and preserved not by
political and military might but by the power of God's
word and Holy Spirit.

Progenitor of the Church

Israel's reconstitution in the deportation and Diaspora
carried far-reaching consequences. Where the adventure
into nation-state life ended in deportation and threatened
Israel's extinction, its reconstitution as a community of
Torah and synagogue served to preserve this community of
faith for 2,500 years. Not enough Christians are aware
that this "culture of the synagogue . . . the most fundamental sociological innovation in the history of religions"
(Yoder 1997, 71) is the prototype of the church, and the
basic reason the church too has survived for 2,000 years
despite the rise and fall of nations and empires. The
Gentile church we see emerging in the Acts of the Apostles
is a copy and continuation of Diaspora Judaism. Israel's
faith survived in the dispersion not just in spite of the
absence of state support but because it got disentangled from
state support.

The popular modern Christian view of Israel and
Judah's exile as a tragedy is in some measure the legacy of
Constantinianism. European state church arrangements
and German, British, and American nationalisms and
patriotisms incline many modern readers of the Bible to see
the exile as only an interim. According to the popular
conviction of too many modern readers, the Davidic state

represents the culmination of God's purposes for his people, which may explain the too-uncritical support by many Christians today for the modern state of Israel. The International Christian Embassy is one indicator that this view is alive in the United States today.[12]

This notion of the exile as merely an interruption in the monarchy is bolstered also by the assumption—for many Americans a dogma—that the nation-state is the highest form of human existence. Witness the many voices calling for the United States to get out of the United Nations. It is ironic that many of these conservative voices are Christians who claim allegiance to Christ, the Lord of a worldwide church. But their view sees the church too as only an interim until God will establish Christ's rule again on the model of the Davidic monarchy.

The biblical narrative sees the exile and dispersion as broadening Judaism's vision to make it an international community itself and to make it a witness that generated converts in nearly all places where Jews lived. It also produced a vision of God's loving kindness for all humankind and a desire for the salvation of all humankind. All in all, the refining experience of exile brought Israel/Judaism closer to what God intended it to be in the first place—a light to the nations.

Reading the Bible as a canon in which the Old Testament story segues into the New Testament, we Christians are obliged to see the exile and dispersion not as a tragedy but rather as a divinely purposed discipline to recall Israel to its true identity and mission. Israel's new calling did not demand forfeiture of its love for the land but recognition of the true way to sanctify the land and extend that sanctification to ever wider areas of earth. The exile moved forward God's purposes in salvation geography.

— 5 —
Jesus: Inheriting the Earth

IN HIS BOOK *The Gospel and The Land* (1974) W. D. Davies offers a thorough review of the importance of the land for Israel. When he comes to Jesus and the New Testament he suggests we should therefore expect to find a concern for that subject. "The hope for the land—sometimes called a 'dogma of Judaism'—could not but have engaged the earliest Christians," he suggests. "To overlook the emphasis on the land in Judaism is to overlook one of the most persistent and passionately held doctrines with which the early church had to come to terms" (5).

And yet, says Davies, "Jesus, as far as we can gather, paid little attention to the relationship between Yahweh and Israel and the land" (365). For the early church Jesus took the place of the temple, says Davies. Or it claimed the church was the temple of the Holy Spirit. Or "the New Testament finds holy space wherever Christ is or has been" (369). Holy land and holy places are spiritualized in the Gospel of John and the letter to the Hebrews, claims Davies: "We refer to the transference of the Christian hope from the earthly Jerusalem, the quintessence of the land in Judaism, to the heavenly" (162).

As for the apostle Paul, although he "never completely and consciously and emotionally abandoned the geography of eschatology" as we see from his pilgrimage to Jerusalem, he "no longer had any need of it," says Davies (220). Given Paul's message to the Gentiles, "The rapid spread of Christianity into the Gentile world carried with it the demotion of the question of the land, even though that question did not die out entirely" (370). In general "we [discover] in the New Testament . . . a growing recognition that the Christian faith is, in principle, cut loose from the land, that the gospel demanded a breaking out of its territorial chrysalis" (336).

Walter Brueggemann in *The Land* (1972) pays his respects to Davies but comes to different conclusions. He claims "that the land theme is more central [in early Christianity] than Davies believes and that it has not been so fully spiritualized as he concludes" (170). In fact, "the coming of Jesus is understood with reference to new land arrangements" (171). "The Jesus movement is indeed the next moment on the way from exile to land" (168), a point made also by Tom Wright: The work of Jesus effects the "real return of Yahweh to Zion," as a consequence of which "Yahweh is now to be king of all the earth." But the way to "restored land" is "restored human beings" (Wright, 428-30). The Magnificat, for example, predicts a reversal for the high and the lowly, which will be a fulfillment of the promise that God made "to Abraham and to his descendants forever" (Luke 1:55). In any reference to Abraham every devout Jew would think first of all of the promise of the land. So also in Jesus's encounter with Zacchaeus: "Today salvation has come to this house, because he too is a son of Abraham" (Luke 19:9). "Jesus's ministry affirms that the land promise is still in effect for this seemingly rejected heir" (Brueggemann, 173). "While the Abraham image undoubtedly is transformed, it is inconceivable that it should have been emptied of its reference to land," says Brueggemann (177). As for Davies' suggestion that holy land and holy places are "spiritualized" in the New Testament (in Hebrews, for example), Brueggemann says, "It is sobering for New Testament exegesis to recognize that [in Hebrews] the single central symbol for the promise of the gospel is land" (Heb chaps. 3 and 4), as signified in the statement to the Hebrews that in Christ they have entered into their "rest" (179), a term that recalls five references in Joshua and four in Judges to the Hebrews finding "rest" after the conflicts involved in settlement in the land.

According to Peter Walker "both Jesus and Paul were working in a climate of articulate Jewish nationalism, which drew much of its rationale from the prophetic scriptures concerning the restoration of Israel and the land. If this is so, it becomes impossible to suggest that the issue of the land passed them by, that they were hardly aware of it. On the contrary, this would have been an integral part of the theological map with which they needed to wrestle. If then their teaching gives . . . the initial impression of dealing little with the land, this is far more likely an indication that they have now consciously processed this issue such that it appears in different forms—not that they have never considered it in the first place" (Johnson and Walker, 115).

Jesus Addresses the Subject

It is not the case, then, that a theme at the very heart of Israel's faith evaporates into spiritualization in the rise of Christianity. We find that Jesus did in fact address the subject, though in ways appropriate to his time, not necessarily in terms current during the conquest (such as we see in Deuteronomy and Joshua), nor in terms current during the period of the monarchy and early exile, nor in the kind of ways we might be looking for today. And because Jesus did not address the subject in ways we might expect, we may quite possibly have missed it. The question is whether Jesus speaks in terms of our preconceptions or whether we let Jesus define the issues.

Jewish people at the time of Jesus lived in the land and, despite the Roman occupation, had considerable self-determination in the operation of the temple, the administration of local synagogues, and the oversight of Jewish halakhic life in general. Jews of Jesus's time were also wrestling with questions raised by Diaspora Judaism— how to relate to Gentile society as a minority within it. Jesus, like his Jewish compatriots, never anticipated Jewish abandonment of the promise of the land or lack of appreciation for its holy places, though his words may have intimated another exile, as we will see.

So if Jesus was not speaking a great deal about the land directly, neither were any other Jews of the time, whether high priestly Sadducees, Pharisees, Essenes, or Zealots, although all of them were in their own way trying to cope with the problems just mentioned—namely, how to define and how to realize the rule of God and how to deal with the Roman occupation that they felt obstructed that rule. The big question was the "restoration"—when it would come, how to achieve it, and above all, what form it would or should take.

What was it then that Jesus did speak to? Chiefly the important issues his fellow Jews were concerned about— namely, how the temple service should be conducted (an issue for the Qumran community also); how his people should live life in obedience to Torah (a central concern of especially the Pharisees); how the Jewish community should relate to the Roman occupation and to the Gentile world in general in an increasingly international and cosmopolitan age; above all, how to exercise faith and obedience toward God to gain Israel's restoration.

In one important respect, however, Jesus, with John the Baptist, moved beyond the horizons of many of his fellow Jews on the subject of where Israel stood on God's eschatological calendar and what that implied for not only a position toward the Roman occupation but for the salvation of the Gentile world as a whole. Having grown up in "Galilee of the Gentiles," Jesus took a definite position on what Jewish attitudes to Gentiles should be. And what he said therefore has quite definite implications for the subject of the land. We will look at several pertinent texts presently.

The Jewish World Mission

First, though, we must notice a phenomenon of Jesus's day that Gentile Christianity has not sufficiently noticed or else has forgotten. "Jesus came upon the scene in the midst of what was par excellence the missionary age of Jewish history," says Joachim Jeremias in his book, *Jesus' Promise to the Nations* (1958, 12). Jewish missionary zeal was intense, and it encountered a religious longing in the Hellenistic world. The Jewish mission facilitated the passage of Gentiles from heathenism into the Jewish community, and the success of the mission was extraordinary. "Jesus grew up in the midst of a people actively engaged, both by the spoken and written word, in a Gentile mission whose impelling motive was a profound sense of their obligation to glorify their God in the Gentile world" (17).

Given this extensive Jewish mission to the Gentiles, we find it surprising that Jesus apparently did not join it but instead seemed to deliberately restrict his mission to his own people. To his disciples he said, "Go nowhere among the Gentiles, and enter no town of the Samaritans, but go rather to the lost sheep of the house of Israel" (Matt 10:5-6). And to the Canaanite woman in the district of Tyre and Sidon he said, "I was sent only to the lost sheep of the House of Israel" (Matt 15:24), though he was persuaded to heal the woman's daughter. The reference in each of these sayings to the lost sheep of the house of Israel may help to explain the harshest saying we hear from Jesus about Judaism's proselytizing mission: "But woe to you, scribes and Pharisees, hypocrites! For you cross sea and land to make a single convert, and you make a new convert twice as much a child of hell as yourselves" (Matt 23:15).

From other texts we could cite, it appears that Jesus was not against outreach to the Gentile world as such. Indeed, he anticipated, if not announced, the appearance of the messianic age, which was expected to see the massive ingathering of Gentiles promised in the prophets. But he seemed to have felt the need of a reform and spiritual renewal of Israel as a prerequisite to this ingathering of Gentiles.

At the opening of Jesus's ministry, in his sermon in the synagogue of his home town of Nazareth, he spoke on the familiar text of Isaiah 61:1-2, "The spirit of the LORD is upon me . . . to bring good news to the poor . . . to proclaim release to the captives and recovery of sight to the blind, to let the oppressed go free, to proclaim the year of the Lord's favor" (Luke 4:18-19). The Matthew and Mark versions of this event state that his hearers were "astonished" or shocked at his message and "took offense at him." The reason, it appears, was that he left off the last phrase of Isaiah 61:2 about "the day of vengeance of our God." The Roman occupation of the land of Israel at the time of Jesus had generated such hatred of Romans among the Jews that for Jesus even to remove the hope and expectation of vengeance upon the Gentiles incurred the hostility of the people of his home town. "No Gentile will have a part in the world to come," said Rabbi Eliezer ben Hyrcanus at the end of the first century of the Christian era (Jeremias, 40-41).

This interpretation finds support in Luke's report of the ending of Jesus's sermon in Nazareth. In the continuation of his sermon Jesus noted that "there were many widows in Israel in the time of Elijah, when . . . there was a severe famine over all the land; yet Elijah was sent to none of them except a widow at Zarephath in Sidon. There were also many lepers in Israel in the time of the prophet Elisha, and none of them was cleansed except Naaman the Syrian" (Luke 4:25-27). This explains why "all in the synagogue were filled with rage . . . [and] drove him out of the town, and led him to the brow of the hill . . . so that they might hurl him off the cliff" (vv. 28-29). "But," says Luke, "he passed through the midst of them."

Passages such as Isaiah 43:5-7 and Psalm 107:2-3 "seemingly referred to a future 'restoration' of Jewish people to the land from the four quarters of the globe." But Jesus read these texts as the ingathering of the Gentiles. "The longed-for 'end of exile' [would be] brought about when people of all nations came into the kingdom of God" (Johnson and Walker, 109).

In spite of Jesus's statement that he "was sent only to the lost sheep of the house of Israel," he did on a few occasions receive Gentiles. According to Matthew 8:5-13 he healed the servant of a centurion at Capernaum, in the course of which he said, "I tell you, many will come from the east and from the west and will eat with Abraham and Isaac and Jacob in the kingdom of heaven, while the heirs of the kingdom will be thrown into outer darkness where there will be weeping and gnashing of teeth." "When Jesus heals," says Jeremias, "his act has eschatological significance, and is always the sign and pledge of the breaking in of the messianic age, an anticipatory participation in its blessings" (Jeremias, 28), in this instance a sign of salvation coming to the Gentiles.

A New Kind of Kingdom

In what is usually called the triumphal entry of Jesus into Jerusalem, celebrated in our churches on Palm Sunday, he offered himself to his people as a "peace candidate," if we can use that modern term, at a time when there were no democratic elections. Whatever the makeup of the crowd that acclaimed him (were they Galileans?), what is important about the event and its circumstances is his rejection of any "Davidic" kind of platform. Taking its cue from Isaiah 62:11 and Zechariah 9:9, the crowd proclaimed, "Tell the daughter of Zion, Look, your king is coming to you, humble, and mounted on a donkey and on a colt, the foal of a donkey." Every hearer of that time would be expected to recall the rest of the text in Zechariah, "He will cut off the chariot from Ephraim and the warhorse from Jerusalem; and the battle bow shall be cut off, and he shall command peace to the nations; his dominion shall be from sea to sea, and from the River to the ends of the earth." No question about a territorial reference here.

With these words and actions Jesus rejected the option of violent or armed conflict with Rome or with anyone else in his proposal for how Israel could or should realize the rule of God in the messianic age. Jesus rejected a restoration of a Davidic kind of nation-state in favor of a universalization of salvation.

In this connection we might note that nowhere in his public ministry did Jesus appeal to or identify with David's career or David's successful conquests, even though David was called a man after God's own heart (1 Sam 13:14; Acts

13:22). The Gospel writers invoke the name of King David in the Matthew and Luke genealogies; Jesus mentions David's act of eating sanctified bread (1 Sam 21:1-6); he refers to David's words in Psalm 110:1 in controversy with his detractors (Matt 12:3; Matt 22:41-46); the public speculates whether Jesus is the son of David (Matt 12:23); and needy persons appeal to Jesus as "Son of David" in beseeching him for healing (Matt 9:27; 20:30-31). But in none of these mentions of David in the Gospels do we find Jesus proposing to restore a Davidic kind of kingdom. Even in the "triumphal entry" where Jesus is acclaimed "Son of David" the text explains that he is riding on a donkey, not on a war horse, and cites the Isaiah and Zechariah texts that predict a messianic age of peace, and a universal one at that, "from the sea to the end of the earth," not a Davidic kingdom from Dan to Beer Sheba.

Furthermore, both Peter's Pentecost sermon (Acts 2) and James's pronouncement at the Jerusalem conference (Acts 15:16-17) decisively clarify in what sense the apostles claim that Jesus fulfilled those promises and hopes revolving around the name of King David. "After this I will return, and I will rebuild the dwelling of David, which has fallen; from its ruins I will rebuild it, and I will set it up, so that all other peoples may seek the Lord, even all the Gentiles over whom my name has been called."

The Problem of the Temple

The much discussed account of what is traditionally called the cleansing of the temple also speaks to important issues of salvation geography. We must remember that this demonstration occurred in the court of the Gentiles. Many Gentiles came on pilgrimage to Jerusalem along with devout Jews but were not allowed to go beyond this outermost court. (Readers who wish to see a sketch of the floor plan of Herod's Temple and its courts may consult *The Interpreter's Dictionary of the Bible,* vol. 4, p. 556.) At gates leading to the inner courts—one for Jewish women and a still further one for Jewish men only—Jewish authorities posted signs chiseled in rock that said, "No man of alien race is to enter within the balustrade and fence that goes around the temple, and if anyone is taken in the act, let him know that he has himself to blame for the penalty of death that follows" (William Barclay's translation, *The Acts of the Apostles,* 1976, 157. A picture of such a rock inscription, found by archaeologists, can be found at <http://www.bible-history.com/archaeology/israel/temple-warning.html>). "Even the Romans took this so seriously that they allowed the Jews to carry out the death penalty for this crime," says Barclay. Therefore the only aspects of Jewish temple worship that Gentiles interested in Jewish faith got exposed to were the sights, sounds, and smells of vendors in the largest outer court hawking doves and lambs for sacrifice. As for the money changers, worshippers could not bring Roman currency into the temple because it bore the image of Caesar and carried the inscription, "Caesar, son of the divine Augustus," and was thus considered idolatrous and defiling. It therefore had to be exchanged for the silver coin of Tyre. The exchange rate was most likely set by the Sanhedrin.

These observations provide the background to Jesus's pronouncement, "Is it not written, 'My house shall be called a house of prayer for all the nations'? But you have made it a den of robbers" (Mark 11:17, quoting from Isa 56:7 and Jer 7:11). Jesus thus protested the exclusion of Gentile worshipers from God's house and condemned the extortionist exchange rate set by the temple priesthood.

I do not agree with the view now popular among some New Testament scholars (for example, Tom Wright) that the so-called cleansing of the temple was actually a symbolic destruction. Instead, Jesus was pointing in the direction of the right use of the temple; "reform" may be too mild a term. It was the Jewish rejection of the way of Jesus that led to the destruction of the temple, and Jesus predicted it, but his temple action was a summons to the divinely intended operation of the temple, for it to be open to Gentiles.

While Jesus may not have said much about Gentiles in the course of his ministry, this momentous saying at the end of his ministry about the temple being a house of prayer for all the nations points in the direction that we see the messianic movement taking in the book of Acts. The public ministry of Jesus was intended to call the Jewish community to move into the messianic age, a major feature of which would be the ingathering of Gentiles. If Jesus was the Christ, as the earliest Christian community confessed, then it was time for the doors of faith to be opened to the Gentiles, as the Old Testament itself anticipated and the Jerusalem conference of Acts 15 claimed.

The Problem of Rome

Equally freighted with import is the saying of Jesus on paying taxes to Caesar. Note the setting. Agents of both Pharisees and Herodians came to Jesus, saying, "Teacher, we know that you are sincere, and teach the way of God in accordance with truth, and show deference to no one; for you do not regard people with partiality. Tell us, then, what you think. Is it lawful to pay taxes to the emperor, or not?" (Matt 22:16-17). The reference is to the tax that the Romans had imposed in the year 6 C.E. We know that the intent of these interrogators was to corner Jesus with the dilemma: If he said to pay, he would be discredited by the overwhelming majority of the population, which was hostile toward the Roman occupation and its taxation. If he said not to pay, he could be reported to Rome as subversive.

Most commentators on this text do not catch the meaning or importance of the next remark, Jesus's request, "Show me the coin used for the tax" (v. 19). His questioners obliged: "And they brought him a denarius," a silver coin about the size of the American dime. The superscription on the Roman denarius read, "Tiberius Caesar Augustus, son of the divine Augustus." As already noted, Jews considered this image of Caesar and the inscription on the Roman currency idolatry, which it was. In producing a coin in response to the request of Jesus, those seeking to trap him were exposed as users of this currency. Not only were their hands defiled by the handling of this coin, but in their use of it they disclosed their own cooperation with the occupation.

We cannot prove the point from silence, but my hunch is that Jesus and his disciples may not have used the Roman currency. It may have been possible for conscientious Jews at the time to have gotten along without using it.

Whatever our conclusion on that question, it is surprising to hear Jesus not condemning his opponents for their own now exposed hypocrisy but saying, "Give therefore to Caesar the things that are Caesar's, and to God the things that are God's" (v. 21). The import of these much debated words is also usually misunderstood. The typical commentary has Jesus advising his hearers—and us—to show an even-handed loyalty to and support for church and state. The point, however, is rather Jesus's shocking "and."

"Give to the emperor what is the emperor's *or* to God what is God's" is what hearers would have expected. In their thinking it was *either* Caesar *or* God. It could not be both. To be obedient to God meant tax resistance, if not outright revolt to somehow expel the Romans. On the other hand, to pay the tax was to acquiesce in the Roman occupation and make the coming of the kingdom of God impossible, in that Roman law interfered with the observance of Mosaic Torah, at least in the minds of many devout Jews. "Eliezer ben Hyrcanus, one of the great rabbis of the Jamnia period, is reported to have spoken of the destruction of Rome as a precondition of the kingdom of Israel's God, as predicted in Zechariah" (Tom Wright, *The New Testament and the People of God*, 1992, 197). Note too the conflict between Roman law and Mosaic law in the story of the woman taken in adultery (John 4), when some Jewish leaders also attempted to catch Jesus in a dilemma. Torah commanded stoning for adultery; Rome reserved the right to impose the death penalty, and adultery was not likely a capital crime in Roman administration at the time.

Rome *or* God? The scandalous "and" in Jesus's ruling could mean only one thing: the Roman occupation was not an insuperable obstacle to the coming of the messianic age in the hearts and lives, individually and corporately, of those willing to receive it. The rule of God could come into being among the Jewish people as a present reality in spite of the presence of Rome, strange as that may sound to modern Christians influenced by dispensationalist teaching.

With the foregoing review of pertinent texts concerning the ministry of Jesus we can begin to catch the logic of Joachim Jeremias' assessment. "Jesus limited his activity to Israel, and during his lifetime forbade his disciples to overstep the boundaries of Israel." And yet "he promised the Gentiles a permanent and unrestricted part in the kingdom of God." We are therefore seeing "two successive events, first the call to Israel, and subsequently the redemptive incorporation of the Gentiles in the kingdom of God" (71).

Therefore when Jesus announced that the kingdom of heaven was at hand, he envisioned the marks of this social order to be not only the quality of life described in the Sermon on the Mount and elsewhere but also the inclusion of Gentiles, which according to prophetic predictions would be, as already noted, one of the consequences of the advent of the messianic age.

According to Jeremias Jesus sought a spiritual renewal of Israel to prepare the way for the Gentile ingathering expected in the messianic age. Moreover, he did not envisage the new era of Israel's renewal and Gentile accession as some distant and improbable event but rather as something imminent and realizable, "at hand," because "the time was fulfilled." God's hour for Israel—*and* for the Gentiles—had arrived.

Jewish Rejection of the Messianic Age

Since the majority of the Jewish community of Jerusalem did not accept Jesus's invitation to move into the new age, Jesus made several serious predictions of the fate of Jerusalem and the destruction of the temple. According to Luke 19:41-44 Jesus wept over the city at the end of the triumphal entry, saying, "If you . . . had only recognized on this day the things that make for peace! But now they are hidden from your eyes. Indeed, the days will come upon you, when your enemies will set up ramparts around you and surround you. . . . They will crush you to the ground, you and your children within you, and they will not leave one stone upon another; because you did not recognize the time of your visitation from God."

According to Matthew 23:37-38 Jesus said, "Jerusalem, Jerusalem, the city that kills the prophets and stones those who are sent to it! How often have I desired to gather your children as a hen gathers her brood under her wings, and you were not willing! See, your house is left to you, desolate." And, according to Mark 13:1-4, as Jesus left the temple and one of his disciples drew attention to the "large stones" and "large buildings" of Herod's temple, he replied, "Not one stone will be left here upon another; all will be thrown down."

Surprised at this prediction, the disciples asked, "Tell us, when will this be, and what will be the sign that all these things are about to be accomplished?" which led Jesus into the discourse usually called the synoptic apocalypse. That discourse concludes in Matthew 24:34 with the words, "Truly I tell you, this generation will not pass away until all these things have taken place." Most commentators rightly take these words to be a prediction of what in fact happened in the war of 66-70 C.E., when Jewish zealots precipitated a revolt during the Passover of 66, which led to the Roman siege of the city and the collapse and destruction of Jerusalem four years later. The story is told in considerable detail in Josephus, who estimates that perhaps one million people were in the city when the siege began. When it ended, many had perished from starvation or violence, many were crucified in reprisals, and most were sold into slavery.

Some critics claim that Jesus's predictions are words attributed to him by the gospel writers after the revolt. My reading persuades me that even if the wording is not a transcript from shorthand or a tape recording of what Jesus said, it reflects a prediction that Jesus in fact made, one in which he echoed the warnings of Old Testament prophets that political folly in not recognizing God's signals in salvation history would again spell disaster. Like Amos, Jesus predicted that the "day of the Lord" "would have surprising and drastic consequences for Israel"

(Johnson and Walker, 103). Once again the land would vomit out its inhabitants. If Jeremias is right, Jesus lamented a Jerusalem that missed its calling, that missed its reading of God's eschatological hour, that missed its chance to be the instrument of a phenomenal ingathering of the Gentiles, although in the providence of God the extension of salvation to the Gentiles happened anyway through the minority of Jews who did confess Jesus as Messiah.

Evidently Jesus himself did not expect the coming judgment upon Jerusalem and the destruction of the temple to preclude this ingathering of Gentiles. Matthew 28:19 has the risen Christ saying to the apostles, "Go therefore and make disciples of all nations, baptizing them in the name of the Father and of the Son and of the Holy Spirit, teaching them to obey everything that I have commanded you."

We can see then that Jesus offers a thoroughly Jewish reading of his heritage in discerning God's purposes for Israel as more than their return to the land from exile—if such return meant a return to the social, political and religious life that the prophets condemned during the time of the Davidic monarchy, and if return meant a return to wars with Gentile nations surrounding such a restored Israel.

True restoration required both a spiritual renewal of Israel *and* the salvation of the pagan world in order to put an end to their attacks upon Israel and Israel's attacks upon them, and an end to wars of Gentile nations upon each other. The Messiah's global reign would assure any Jew who desired it the privilege of seeking to live between Dan and Beer Sheba, but would make residence anywhere else equally inviting, seeing that the entire world had been given to Abraham, that the entire world was now Messiah's realm, and that all parts of the entire world were in principle, or at least potentially, holy (Rom 4:13.

This will be discussed more fully in the following chapter).

As any careful reading of the Jewish Scriptures makes clear, the view that Israel's salvation should and would embrace the Gentiles in the messianic age was not original with Jesus. Nor the related view that the promise of the land to Abraham extended to the whole world. Even the view that Israel's and the world's salvation called for the abandonment of Jewish nationalist aspirations and their attendant violence is not original with Jesus, as the triumphal entry and Zechariah text quoted there show. So also the most well-known statement of Jesus about possession of land, his statement in the beatitudes that the meek shall inherit the earth. Although many Christians may consider the beatitudes as novel with Jesus, an idealistic departure from Old Testament realism, this text too is already present in the Jewish Scriptures. It appears, in fact, as practically a refrain in Psalm 37.

It is worth printing the relevant verses from Psalm 37 here. "Trust in the LORD, and do good; so you will dwell in the land, and enjoy security. . . . For the wicked shall be cut off; but those who wait for the LORD shall inherit the land. . . . But the meek shall inherit the land, and delight themselves in abundant prosperity. . . . For those blessed by the LORD shall inherit the land, but those cursed by him shall be cut off. . . . The righteous shall inherit the land, and dwell upon it for ever. . . . Wait for the LORD, and keep to his way, and he will exalt you to inherit the land" (vv. 3, 9, 11, 22, 29, 34).

What may be identified as original with Jesus is his announcement in his sermon in Nazareth (Luke 4) that the rule of God is "at hand" and his conviction that both the "restoration" of Israel *and* the extension of salvation to the Gentiles required his passion, death, and resurrection. It is tragedy and irony—and glory—that although "Jesus

. . . rejected the literalistic (or, we might even say, 'Zionist')" interpretation of Israel's restoration and had "diagnosed the disease of Jewish nationalism and publicly distanced himself from it, [he] at last allowed the consequence of that disease to fall upon him. . . . Although Jesus was not a proto-Zealot . . . he was prepared to end up on a Roman cross on the false charge of being just such a nationalist" (Johnson and Walker, 113, 119).

We must conclude that "the apparent silence of the New Testament must not be construed as . . . ignorance or lack of concern about the unfulfilled promise concerning the land." Jesus "offers us an alternative, seldom tried but well worth following. And into this situation he speaks with a refreshingly different voice, which we need to obey" (Johnson and Walker, 118-119).

— 6 —
The Apostolic Church: To the Ends of the Earth

THE BOOK OF ACTS reports how the apostolic church gradually came to understand the intentions of Jesus and to engage in the Christian world mission. Therewith Jesus's hope and expectation of a Gentile ingathering was fulfilled, at first on a small scale but then with growing momentum.

The apostles were not immediately open to the inclusion of Gentiles. We see a period of hesitation before they reached clarity on the matter. The two disciples on the road to Emmaus (Luke 24:13-32) say to the risen but as yet unrecognized Jesus, "We had hoped that he was the one to redeem Israel," insinuating that the public ministry of Jesus had looked promising to them but that Jesus had not restored Israel according to their preconceptions. And Acts 1:6-8 reports the gathered disciples asking the risen Jesus, "Lord, is this the time when you will restore the kingdom to Israel?" To which Jesus replies, "It is not for you to know the times or periods that the Father has set by his own authority. But you will receive power when the Holy Spirit has come upon you; and you will be my witnesses in Jerusalem, in all Judea and Samaria, and to the ends of the earth."

Jesus's answer may appear to avoid the disciples' question or suggest its irrelevance. Actually his reply is a most appropriate answer, and it makes good sense in Jewish terms. In tactful words Jesus is telling his disciples, "Your understanding of restoration is wrong." Possibly referring to Hosea 6:2, "On the third day he will raise us up," Jesus explains that Israel has been restored in [his] resurrection, and the apostles will be witnesses of this fact from Jerusalem to the ends of the earth. "The restored kingdom of Israel is the world coming under the rule of Israel's true king" (Johnson and Walker, 107-08). In other words, restoration is not scattered Israel's return to the land for still another round of politics and military adventures as usual, but an extension of Israel's inheritance to "the ends of the earth," bringing the whole human race under the reign of Messiah, the prince of peace.

There were two ways at the time (and there still are) of seeking restoration, that is, an end to Israel's exile. One was to bring all Jews back to an independent nation within the traditional boundaries of the promised land—at the risk of resumed conflict with other nations. The other was to remove all boundaries in favor of a sanctification of the whole earth. Then, as now, most Jews were not ready to return to a violent and zealot-inclined Israel, and most Jews within the boundaries of Israel's historic homeland were unwilling to accept the vision of a universalized reign of God, although the (Jewish) apostolic community came to see with increasing clarity that the appearance of the messianic age meant the beginning of the salvation and sanctification of the whole earth.

Jesus's answer to the question of the disciples in Acts 1 can also be interpreted to imply what Paul spells out in his letter to the Romans: (1) There is an unfinished agenda God has with ethnic Israel, but that is God's business.

(2) This unfinished agenda is not, however, an obstacle to God's *other* agenda—to extend salvation to the Gentiles. The restoration of the kingdom includes the ingathering of Gentiles from the ends of the earth and thus salvation to the ends of the earth. In fact, Jesus's answer can be taken to say that with the completion of his messianic mission the process of restoration is inaugurated, although the timetable of the process is in God's hands. Jesus's words may also be taken to mean that the incorporation of Gentiles was possible even if the "restoration" of Israel may not have happened according to the apostles' original hopes or expectations.

A New Paradigm of Restoration

According to the revised understanding of the apostles reflected in Peter's Pentecost sermon, the restoration of the kingdom actually did happen. Acts 2:36 indicates how the apostolic church soon grasped Jesus's redefinition of the kingdom and saw the resurrection and ascension as the fulfillment of that expectation. "Therefore let the entire house of Israel know with certainty that God has made him both Lord and Messiah, this Jesus whom you crucified." God reversed the judgment of the Sanhedrin and of Pilate, vindicated Jesus, and enthroned him at the right hand of God.

Stephen's unusually long address in Acts 7 offers further confirmation of the apostolic church's revised understanding of restoration. A deacon appointed to care for neglected Hellenist widows, Stephen may have been a Hellenist himself, sympathetic to Hellenists, and thus holding the more liberal view of Diaspora Judaism toward Gentiles. In his defense before the Jerusalem council Stephen rehearses the pre-monarchic era of Israel's history, holding up the examples of Israel's ancient heroes, Abraham, Joseph, and Moses. His speech "highlights the way God had revealed his holy presence and divine [salvation] outside the land" (Johnson and Walker, 97). Not incidentally, Stephen's reference to these ancient worthies "prepares the way thematically for the dispersal of the believers from Jerusalem recorded in the next chapter" (Johnson and Walker, 97).

What might surprise any observant reader is that Stephen abruptly breaks off his recital of Israel's history of salvation with a deprecating reference to Solomon's construction of the temple. "Yet the Most High does not dwell in houses made with human hands; as the prophet says, 'Heaven is my throne, and earth my footstool. What kind of house will you build for me, says the Lord, or what is the place of my rest? Did not my hand make all these things?'" (Acts 7:48-50). With that Stephen breaks into fierce accusation, "You stiff-necked people, uncircumcised in heart and ears, you are forever opposing the Holy Spirit . . . . Your ancestors . . . killed those who foretold the coming of the Righteous One, and now you have become his betrayers and murderers" (vv. 51-52). For Stephen the monarchy and the nation-state were Israel's big mistake, its apostasy. And the temple unfortunately became the central symbol of this mistake—state religion and the exclusion of Gentiles. This misuse of the temple is what Jesus condemned. The temple authorities, of course, were the ones who had turned Jesus over to the Romans for execution.

In the course of the apostolic mission the doors of faith were duly opened to Gentiles, first to the Ethiopian, then to the Samaritans, then to the household of Cornelius, and then to all believing Gentiles at an accelerated pace in the Pauline mission. The Jerusalem conference reported in Acts 15:6-29 reached a decisive consensus, and it was predicated upon the conviction that the messianic age had indeed come. "I will rebuild the dwelling of David, which has fallen; from its ruins I will rebuild it . . . so that all other peoples may seek the Lord—even all the Gentiles over whom my name has been called" (vv. 16-17). The logic was simple and clear: if the messianic age had dawned, then it was time to offer salvation to Gentile believers and to receive them as Gentiles, not necessarily as proselytes to Judaism, although full conversion to Judaism was open to anyone who chose it: "For in every city, for generations past, Moses has had those who proclaim him, for he has been read aloud every Sabbath in the synagogues" (v. 21). That is, not only could Jews continue to practice circumcision, maintain food laws, and keep the Sabbath, but also any Gentiles who chose to convert to Judaism completely were free to do so. As also the apostle Paul spells out in his letter to the Romans, the extension of salvation to Gentiles and their ingathering did not erase Jewish identity or prevent Jewish observance of Torah. Paul encourages both Jews and Gentiles not to try to change their identity, Gentiles getting circumcised or Jews trying to remove the marks of circumcision (1 Cor 7:18). Paul is consistent in this, even having the Jew Timothy circumcised (Acts 16:3).

God Gave Abraham the Cosmos

It is clear that Paul, the apostle to the Gentiles, shared the apostolic faith's view of the land. In Romans 4:13 Paul states that in the promise of the land God was giving Abraham and all his descendants the world (Greek "kosmos"). And in Galatians 3:14 Paul says "that in Christ Jesus the blessing of Abraham might come to the Gentiles." If the primary blessing to Abraham was land, this logic implied the promise of a divinely provided home for Gentiles too. Paul doesn't seem to feel the need to argue the cosmic dimension of the promise to Abraham. He accepts this belief as a given and as understood by his readers, making it the premise for his argument about the righteousness of faith.

The view that God promised Abraham and his descendants the whole world is not original with Paul. It is found already in writers of Second Temple Judaism. Several of them deserve citation here. Sirach 44.21 says, "Therefore the Lord assured [Abraham] with an oath that the nations would be blessed through his offspring; that he would make him as numerous as the dust of the earth . . . and give them an inheritance from sea to sea and from the Euphrates to the ends of the earth." (This last phrase is part of the text from Zechariah, cited also at the triumphal entry of Jesus.) The apocryphal book of Jubilees says, "And [Abraham] rejoiced because the Lord had given him seed upon the earth to inherit the earth" (17.3), and Jubilees 32.19 says, "And I will give to thy [Jacob] seed all the earth which is under heaven . . . and . . . they shall get possession of the whole earth and inherit it forever" (see also Jubilees 19.21 and Jubilees 22.14.) The Hellenistic Jew Philo of Alexandria writes, applying the global promise to Moses also, "And so, as he [Moses] abjured the accumulation of lucre . . . God rewarded him by giving him instead . . . the wealth of the whole earth and sea and rivers. . . . For since God judged him worthy to appear as partner of His own possessions, He gave into his hands the whole world as a portion well fitted for His heir" (Moses 1.155. See also the Sibylline Oracles 3.767-70, the Apocalypse of Baruch 14.13, and 4th Ezra 6.59).[13]

In the minds of Second Temple era Jews other than Paul the apparently fairly widespread view that the promise to Abraham encompassed "the world" may not have meant what Paul intended by it, although I doubt that the Jews who used this language expected the whole human race to convert to Judaism. In the minds of many of them it may have meant the hope of a return to a Davidic kind of imperial rule out of Jerusalem over the Gentiles.

The "messianic Judaism" of Jesus and Paul did not mean a Davidic kind of imperial rule, of course, but Paul's take on this matter was certainly not novel, because he was (merely?) offering a messianic rationale for a widespread practice already obtaining in many synagogues of the dispersion, as illustrated in Paul's address in Acts 13, where the apostle greets two groups of people, "You Israelites," (v. 13. "Descendants of Abraham's family" in v. 26) and "others who fear God," referring with that second term to Gentile converts who had become worshipers of Israel's God but declined circumcision and perhaps some other Jewish regulations.

We should remember that Paul's time preceded the era after the Jewish wars of 66-70 and 135 C.E., when Judaism became more standardized at the Jewish rabbinic center of Jamnia/Yavneh in Galilee. At the time of Jesus and Paul, Judaism existed in several varieties—Sadducean, Pharisaic, Essene, Zealot, Hellenistic, and Messianic—and it was not yet decided which one would eventually prevail.[14]

We can see, then, that the story of apostolic Christianity bears quite directly upon the subject of the land. The apostolic writings claimed that if Jews thought the land God had promised them was only that territory between Dan and Beer Sheba, they were selling themselves short. God had promised Abraham nothing less than the world—and a salvation whose scope would eventually embrace the world. The apostolic faith did not propose to deny a single Jew the right to live in Israel's historic land, although most Jews at the time, like today, preferred not to. Nor did apostolic faith disparage any degree of devotion to that land and the places in it. All that New Testament faith did was two things: (1) Accept the already existing Jewish view of expanded horizons. Since the promise to Abraham embraced the whole wide world, God was giving Abraham's descendants the right to live anywhere on the face of the earth and sanctify the places where they lived, even while they had the privilege of continuing to show special devotion to the sacred places of their salvation history. (2) Invite Jews to share salvation with Gentiles, which Hellenistic synagogues were already doing, so that Gentiles too would accept responsibility to sanctify the territory in which *they* lived—that is, to live in righteousness, peace, justice, and gratitude in the space they occupied on earth.

Continued Love for the Land of Israel

Neither Jesus nor apostolic Christianity expected Judaism to lose its appreciation of the traditional holy land, nor did they expect Christianity to leave Judaism behind. They instead had every expectation that the Jewish community had a right to reside in and possess its historic homeland and to administer its temple service and synagogue life, subject, of course, to the conditions God laid down in Mosaic Torah in the first place for life in the land. The apostolic Church did not anticipate any loss of devotion to the holy land and holy places.

Although he was an apostle to the Gentiles, Paul made a "collection for the saints" to carry to Jerusalem (1 Cor 16:1-3) because it was fitting for Gentiles "to be of service to them in material things," since Jerusalem was the origin of their "spiritual blessings" (Rom 15:27. See also Gal 2:10). Paul made pilgrimage to Jerusalem, the place of his theological study, and brought the Gentile believer Trophimus with him on his last pilgrimage (Acts 21:27-29). According to Acts 21:17-26, Jewish Christian leaders in Jerusalem persuaded Paul to join four men "under a vow" going "through the right of purification," this to reassure "thousands of believers" who were "zealous for the law" that Paul was not teaching "Jews living among the Gentiles to forsake Moses." In his letter to the Romans (chapters 9–11) Paul argues that the covenant with Israel will never be revoked. I take that to include the promise of the land, broadened, however, to embrace the "cosmos," as Paul puts it in Romans 4:13.

At the same time, Jesus and the apostolic church did not expect the reestablishment of a Davidic Zionist state, a course that would have led to an exclusive community. Instead, they hoped for a renewed Israel that would offer salvation to the nations. They expected a movement incorporating Gentiles into Israel, not a Gentile faith cut off from Judaism and Jerusalem, but one in which Gentile orientation and affections would be directed to Jerusalem. We see that stance clearly in Paul, the apostle to the Gentiles. Jerusalem would thereby become a holy place for Gentiles too, a center without boundaries, the source of the sanctification of the whole earth. Then would be fulfilled what was written by the prophets Micah and Isaiah about people coming up to the mountain of the house of the Lord to learn his law and to study war no more.

It is noteworthy, however, to see in the great commission a kind of reversal of the Isaiah 2/Micah 4 vision of nations coming up to the mountain of the house of the Lord to learn God's law and the way of peace. Although the theme of an outgoing herald is already there in the Old Testament, the great commission in the synoptic Gospels and Acts 1:8 speaks of messengers going *out* to the "nations" (Matt 28:19), "beginning from Jerusalem" (Luke 24:47). It is the Gentile Luke who mentions Jerusalem in both his Gospel and Acts, indicating that the new vision of salvation geography does not forget Jerusalem. The center of salvation history remains, whether nations come up *to* Jerusalem or the message goes out *from* Jerusalem. The coming and going are not mutually exclusive. Both are expected. Each encourages the other.

And yet at a certain point in salvation history and salvation geography, the cause of God's salvation does not continue to just wait for people to come. Solomon in his oration at the dedication of the temple in Jerusalem says, "When a foreigner . . . comes and prays toward this house . . . for they shall hear of your great name" (1 Kings 8:41-42). But Paul says, "How are they to hear without someone to proclaim [the Lord]?" (Rom 10:14). In one sense the great commission, the Christian world mission, is the invitation going out to people to come up to the mountain of the house of the Lord to learn God's law and the way of peace.

Center Without Boundaries

The universalization of salvation makes Jerusalem a center without boundaries rather than the contested political capital of a tiny state. It makes Jerusalem what God intended and still intends it to be, the center and inspiration for a sanctified earth.

We may be perplexed by the mystery of why the Gentile mission exploded despite the fact that only a minority of Jews accepted Messiah Jesus and his concern for Israel's renewal as preparation for the ingathering of the Gentiles. We can see that the Gentile accession, despite the refusal of the majority of Jews to recognize their historic hour, led to one most regrettable consequence—a Gentile Christianity all too soon cut off from its Jewish roots.

We can safely conclude that neither Jesus nor the apostolic Church spiritualized Jewish convictions and hopes about the land, as W. D. Davies says—certainly not in the sense of an otherworldly faith, unrelated to life in time and space. Much better than "spiritualized" would be "universalized." One implication of this is surely that borders (not to mention concrete walls) were not a concern for the Jewish apostolic church, as they also were not for most Diaspora Jews of the time, because neither group of people ever forgot God's promise to Abraham.

Despite its temptation to adopt otherworldly and mystic tendencies to replace earthly realism, Christianity in time also developed an appreciation of the holy places that has led to an extensive modern tourist industry. Christianity has unfortunately not developed an adequate understanding of the importance of the vision of Jesus and the apostolic Church to extend the reach of holy land until it embraces the whole earth.

The New Testament offers a new "sacred geography." "Instead of a static acceptance of the 'holy land' and the 'holy places' of the Old Testament, the New Testament sees . . . a divinely led and empowered geographical strategy [from Jerusalem to Judea . . . to the ends of the earth]. New lands and new places are chosen . . . in such a way as to designate all places on the map as potentially holy" (Janzen, 153).

— 7 —
Gentile Christianity: Desecrating/Sanctifying Land

THE STORY of the post-apostolic Christian church and possession of land is an enormously complex subject: It can refer to the relationship of early Christians to the historic land of Israel, but also to the record of how well or how poorly Christians, almost all of them Gentiles since the time of the apostolic church, have sanctified or failed to sanctify the lands around the world in which they live.

As we can see from the book of Acts, earliest Christianity did not lose its Jewish territorial, geographical rootedness. Even the great commission to get the gospel out to the entire world had its beginning point in Jerusalem. From the limited information available to us we gather that some of the earliest Jewish Christians continued life in the land in observance of Jewish customs. But Jewish Christians of Jerusalem did not support the 66-70 C.E. Jewish war, at the end of which many inhabitants of besieged Jerusalem starved, perished of disease, were executed, or were sold into slavery. Instead Christians, apparently forewarned by the words of Jesus in the

Synoptic Apocalypse (Mark 13 and Matthew/Luke parallels), withdrew to Pella across the Jordan. "[Pella] became an important center of the Church" even after "the return of a large part of the community to Jerusalem after 135" (*Interpreters Dictionary of the Bible*, "Pella"). We might be puzzled by this last comment, seeing that the Roman government banished all Jews from Jerusalem and Judea after suppressing the revolt of Bar Kochba in 135. Were these people who "returned" to Jerusalem Jewish Christians who no longer identified themselves as Jews? Or were these Gentile Christians? We are not told.

Robert Wilken says it was Origen (185-254), the Greek Christian philosopher from Alexandria, who promoted a "spiritualization" of the Christian faith, disconnecting it from geographical realities. Citing Galatians 4:26 about "the Jerusalem above [that] is free" and Hebrews 12:22 about "the heavenly Jerusalem," he tried to show "that when the Scriptures speak of Jerusalem they do not have in mind the city in Judea that was once the capital of the Jewish nation; Jerusalem . . . does not designate a future political center but a spiritual vision of heavenly bliss" (Wilken, 1992, 70). Influential as Origen was, his departure from salvation geography did not last much more than a century. What brought the church's thinking back to earth, although not necessarily in the right way, was the advent of Constantine and his political establishment of Christianity

The Impact of Constantine

Christianity became almost completely non-Jewish after Constantine, who issued his Edict of Toleration in 313 C.E. and convened the noted Council of Nicea in 325, usually remembered for its Creed. Constantine's measures fostered an exponential growth of Gentile Christianity. But

Nicea witnessed another important development. Constantine's mother, Queen Helena, was at the Council, and Bishop Macarius of Jerusalem, the city still called Aelia Capitolina at the time, "reported to her that nothing had been done since the crucifixion to commemorate and preserve the sites where the dramatic events of the last hours of Jesus had been enacted. To do so now, he urged, was surely the greatest act for the furtherance of the new faith that the emperor could perform. Queen Helena was greatly moved by this appeal, and so was [Constantine] when she told him.

"A year later, in A.D. 326, she journeyed to Jerusalem —the name Aelia was subsequently abandoned—and together with Macarius determined the locations where Jesus had been crucified and buried . . . and over them Constantine . . . erected . . . the Church of the Holy Sepulchre, which became the most sacred shrine in Christendom and the focus of Christian pilgrimage.

"The new Church was the most important structure in the city, and indeed, no expense had been spared. In a letter to Macarius commissioning the building, Constantine had written: 'It is fitting that your wisdom do so order and make provision for everything necessary that not only shall this basilica be the finest in the world, but that the details also shall be such that all the fairest structures in every city may be surpassed by it.'

"Eusebius [early church historian] saw the shrine being built and was present at its consecration in 335, and he called it 'a spectacle of surpassing beauty'" (Kolleck and Pearlman, 33-34).

Queen Helena and Bishop Macarius also identified the place in Bethlehem where they believed Jesus had been born, and Constantine erected there, also out of state funds, the Church of the Nativity, which was "second only to the Church of the Holy Sepulchre" (Kolleck and Pearlman, 33-34).

Constantine's architectural commemoration of these historic sites in salvation history sparked a phenomenal growth in Christian pilgrimage. Wealthy Christians, following the example of Constantine, "built monasteries, convents, hospices, churches and chapels in and around Jerusalem and Bethlehem and also in the Judean desert, which had begun to attract hermits" (Kolleck and Pearlman, 33-34). Interest in holy places and pilgrimage to them spread into Galilee as well. According to Robert Wilken, "The number of churches built in the Holy Land during the Christian era [from Constantine until the Muslim conquest] is over five hundred" (Wilken, p. 184).

A Christian Holy Land

Interest in pilgrimage seems to have generated a desire among Christians to actually live in the Holy Land. In the three centuries from Constantine until the Islamic occupation of Jerusalem in 638 the whole country became more or less Christianized and also experienced considerable population growth. One pilgrim, St. Paula of Rome, who made her pilgrimage in 382 and had St. Jerome as her guide, wrote, "In the village of Christ all is rusticity, and, except for psalms, silence. Whithersoever you turn, the ploughman holding the plough-handle sings Alleluyah; the perspiring reaper diverts himself with psalms, and the vine-dresser sings the Songs of David while he trims the vine with curved knife. These are the ballads of the country, these are the love-songs, as they are commonly called. These are whistled by the shepherds and are the implements of the husbandman" (Kolleck and Pearlman, 42, 47). Even allowing for pious embellishment, we see here a favorable description of a Christian society developing in the land.

Wilken cites a population estimate for Jerusalem of 50,000 and a population density for the whole land four times that of biblical times. "Pilgrims, like tourists, were good for business." Quoting Jewish scholar Avi-Yonah, Wilken says, "The stream of capital which then began to flow explains better than any other factor the astonishing prosperity of Palestine in the Byzantine period" (Wilken, 1992, 179).

For Christians too Jerusalem had become a holy place, but now the most sacred site was not the Temple Mount but rather the place of Jesus's cross and tomb. Constantine's erection of the grandest structure in the empire on the site of Christ's burial and resurrection made it, in effect, the Christian "temple," in Christian devotion the substitute for the Jewish temple. After several centuries Jerusalem became without question the holiest place in the affections of Christendom, the destination of massive pilgrimage, the center of many monasteries, and the seat of an influential Bishop.[15]

It seems that the church, like ancient Israel, couldn't resist the temptation to also become a state religion. The emperor Justinian I firmly established Christianity as the state faith, made himself head of the church, and attempted to police orthodoxy. And, as in the first years of the Davidic dynasty, state religion allied with state political and economic and military power exhibited remarkable success in the growth and prosperity of the church.

Christians left the Temple Mount a rubble in order to take a holy delight, it appears, in the fulfillment of predictions by the prophets of divine judgment and destruction upon Jerusalem and the prediction of Jesus in Matthew 23:38 and 24:2 that the temple would be destroyed. This left that site open for the second caliph Omar to clean up the Temple Mount and erect a mosque there, which has given Islam possession of the place of Solomon's and Herod's temples to this day.

Muslim Occupation

When the Muslims occupied Jerusalem in 638 C.E.— without bloodshed, thanks to a surrender negotiated by Sophronius, its Bishop at the time—Christians were dismayed by their loss of power and prestige and, like some Jews after the fall of Jerusalem, expected an early restoration of their fortunes. One writer whom historians call Pseudo-Methodius reflected these apocalyptic hopes and spoke of a "restoration" of Jerusalem, just as Jews did after earlier destructions of Zion. Indeed, he expected a recovery of Byzantine military power and its defeat of the Muslim "infidels" (unbelievers), and thereby the rescue of Jerusalem and the restoration of its status as Christianity's "holy land." Pre-Constantinian Christians had avoided the term "holy land" because it was the vocabulary of Judaism, but had begun to adopt it by the time of the rise of Islam.

The Muslim conquest of the area, beginning in 638, did not immediately change conditions because of Islam's toleration of Christians as "people of the book." But Islamic rule and its policy of treating Christians as "dhimmis" led over the centuries to the Islamicization of the land until in modern times only a minority of Palestinian Arabs has remained Christian.

However, Islam too, especially Palestinian Islam, considered Jerusalem holy, "al Quds" ("the holy," cognate to the Hebrew qodesh), and built not only the Mosque of Omar but also al Aqsa Mosque on the Temple Mount, a space that Christian construction of pilgrimage sites had not preempted.

Muslim control of the holy land eventually had a negative effect on Christian pilgrimage. Sometimes local Muslim rulers hindered or prohibited Christian pilgrimage. The Caliph al-Hakim destroyed the Church of the Holy Sepulcher in 1008 or 1009, "and the brutality encountered during the next several decades by Christians within Palestine and by Pilgrims seeking to visit the holy land was one justification for the Crusades" (March, 22). Beginning around 1076 the Seljuks introduced "a policy of repression against . . . Christians and Jews. Pilgrimage was banned, and Pilgrims who happened to be [in Jerusalem] were gravely maltreated" (Kolleck and Pearlman, 68, 86). And so Pope Urban II proposed a crusade at Clermont in 1095. Responding to this call, the French Crusaders took Jerusalem in 1099 and butchered most of its inhabitants, including women and children, even though many of these inhabitants must surely have been Christians. But the Crusader control of Jerusalem lasted less than 100 years. The resumption of Muslim rule permitted some Christian pilgrimage, but pilgrims complained about conditions such as tolls, fees and other rip-offs for transportation and access to holy places (Kolleck and Pearlman, 157).

All of this changed, of course, with the British takeover of Palestine in 1914 and then the establishment of the state of Israel in 1948. As everyone today knows, these developments, together with modern travel, have triggered an explosion in the tourist industry, although such tourism fluctuates with the rise and fall of violence in the never-ending conflict between Israelis and Palestinians. Already "by the start of the twentieth century, some 5,000 tourists and about 15,000 pilgrims were passing through Jaffa every year. Although welcomed, the Westerners were still known as *franj* or 'Franks,' the old Arab appellation for the Crusaders" (La Guardia, 12).

The Record of Christianity

If this is the record of Gentile Christian life in and pilgrimage to this land, what is the record of Christianity in sanctifying the places elsewhere in the world where it has exercised influence? That story is so large and complicated that we can offer only illustrations. We are obliged to say that, in general, Constantine's establishment of Christianity as a state religion may have helped to produce some idyllic life, such as that described by St. Paula. But it did for Christianity what the rise of the monarchy did for ancient Israel and Judaism. That is, Christianity allied itself with nation-states and endorsed all too many national wars of conquest and defense. Many of these wars took place in Christian Europe, up to and including the Hundred Years' War and World Wars I and II.

Even more disturbing are European conquests beyond the borders of Europe. In 1620, the Puritan colonists of New England "believed they were establishing the New Israel. . . . Promised Land imagery figured prominently in shaping English colonial thought. Pilgrims identified themselves with the ancient Hebrews. They viewed the New World as the New Canaan. They were God's chosen people headed for the Promised Land. . . . This self-image of being God's Chosen People called to establish the New Israel became an integral theme in America's self-interpretation. During the Revolutionary period it emerged with new force. 'We cannot but acknowledge that God hath graciously patronized our cause and taken us under his special care, as he did his ancient covenant people,' Samuel Langdon preached at Concord, New Hampshire in 1788. . . . 'Never was the possession of arms used with more glory, or in a better cause, since the days of Joshua the son of Nun,' Ezra Stiles urged in Connecticut in 1783" (May, 72. Also http://gbgmumc.org/umw/joshua/may7180.stm).

The American appeal to the Hebrew conquest of the Promised Land had shameful consequences. "From the 1820s until the 1840s the Cherokees, Choctaws and other members of the Five Civilized Tribes were expelled from the deep south to Oklahoma. These forced marches to Oklahoma are known as the 'Trail of Tears' because of the disease, suffering, and massive number of deaths the tribes experienced, and the grief they felt in leaving their homes. Some years later (1864) in the far southwest, 8,500 citizens of the Navajo Nation were forced out of their homelands. Their removal to a confinement camp in New Mexico is remembered bitterly as the 'The Long Walk.' Throughout the nineteenth century there were countless military clashes between Native Americans and the U.S. Army supporting white settlers" (May, 72).

The story should be familiar to all Americans. Unfortunately, America has been afflicted with national amnesia on this chapter of its history. Christians have broken treaty after treaty with the native peoples in forcibly taking possession of their land, have instituted policies that have led to the death of much of the Indian population, and have stolen all the best land, besides which American corporations are now discovering mineral resources on Indian reservations and exploiting these as well. Still, America has hypocritically liked to think of itself even today as "the city on a hill" (a Sermon on the Mount phrase President Ronald Reagan liked) and has dotted the national landscape with biblical place names such as Bethany, Bethel, Bethlehem, Canaan, Hebron, Jericho, Kidron, Nazareth, Salem, Shiloh, Zion, and Zoar.

The Spanish and Portuguese conquest of South America is a similarly shameful story. "The conquest of Canaan was the model for their invasion of America. Mexican biblical scholar Elsa Támez explains: The story of the conquest of Canaan is the most often used biblical foundation for the conquest of this continent. Juan Ginés de Sepúlveda [a prominent and influential Spanish philosopher of the 16th century] used this biblical theme to legitimate the war against its inhabitants. . . . He justified the conquest in order to punish blasphemy but also because the continent was a special donation by God, as the promised land. . . . God chose the Spanish to carry out this divine judgment against the infidels, and to conquer their lands. From this Sepúlveda affirmed that such a war besides being licit was necessary because of the gravity of the people's crimes" (May, 76). Sepúlveda, apologist for the Spanish conquests, "cited the many familiar passages from Deuteronomy and Leviticus, detailing the ideal of the violent expulsion of the Canaanites from their land, and their replacement by Israelites, at the behest of God" (Prior, 56).

"Most Spaniards . . . believed in the righteousness of their cause. They also believed that Native Americans were 'naturally wicked.' 'God condemned the whole race of Indians to perish for the horrible sins committed in their paganism,' a priest declared. . . . 'Just as Joshua was willed by God to destroy the people of Canaan because they were idolaters, thus God willed Spain to destroy the Indians'" (May, 76).

To their credit it must be said that some people of conscience such as Bartolomé de las Casas (1474-1566) protested the crimes of the conquistadors against the Native Americans, but those protests did not undo the crimes. Indeed, out of pity for his beloved Native Americans las Casas at first proposed bringing black slaves from Africa instead of enslaving Indians, though las Casas soon enough regretted that suggestion.

Speaking of Africa, not only did Christians engage in

the horrible slave trade (though it was also Christians who abolished that trade), they also seized African land and treated its inhabitants on the model of Deuteronomy and Joshua. The roots of apartheid were "the historical experience of the . . . 'Afrikaners.' Especially important was their sense of divine election. They too understood themselves as God's Chosen People. South Africa was their Promised Land. . . . In 1836 the Afrikaners . . . set out for the Transvaal region in the North to establish their own republic. This movement north became known as the 'Great Trek.'. . . Many Afrikaners died during the trek. Others were killed in battles with Africans. The decisive battle was at Blood River on December 16, 1838. Some 10,000 Zulu warriors attacked the trekkers. Over 3,000 Zulus were killed. No Afrikaners died. The Afrikaners attributed their victory to God's intervention. They said it was a covenant God made with them.

"Land was central to this self-image. An historian explains, 'The very spine of Afrikaner history (no less than the historical sense of the Hebrew Scriptures upon which it is based) involves the winning of "the land" from alien, and indeed evil forces'" (May, 78).

Besides the record of Christians in Europe itself, these mega stories of Christian conquest on three other continents, North and South America and Africa (we have not touched upon Australia or Asia), add up to a desecration of the lands they colonized. Its effect has been the displacement of native peoples, sending many of them in effect into permanent exile from their ancestral lands. Divine retribution may yet descend upon those who have committed these sins.

Some Beacons of Light

Over against the failures of Christian societies to sanc-

tify their lands are counter illustrations, usually small bea-
cons of light that reflect what was modeled by Abraham
and by Jewish synagogues of the exile. One thinks of
monastic communities and convents that already early in
the history of Christianity sought an alternative to the
compromises of an increasingly worldly church. One
thinks also of Moravians fleeing persecution who in 1722
established the town of Herrnhut on Count Nicholas von
Zinzendorf's estate and from there sent out many mission-
aries, some of whom were responsible for John Wesley's
conversion and preaching career. It was the Moravians
who in the early 1770s established the two Christian
Indian towns of Gnadenhütten and Schönbrunn in eastern
Ohio, ninety inhabitants of which were massacred by
Pennsylvania militia on March 8, 1782, in connection with
the Revolutionary war.[16]

America witnessed the establishment of other communities such as the Shakers, the record of whose life, while
unorthodox, is an ongoing benediction to our society, even
though the communities themselves have disappeared.
Their historic sites continue to prod the consciences of
tourists who visit them.

Then too there are many ordinary Christian communities in Canada and the United States, often revolving
around their local congregations. Here people generally
live in peace with one another, offer neighborly help in
time of need, and forget to lock their houses when they go
on errands. Imperfect though they may be, the people of
these communities are spiritual descendants of Abraham
who sanctify the land God has given them as their home.
It has been the philosophy of many Amish and Mennonite
farmers in Pennsylvania and Ohio to leave their land better
than they found it.

Too much of Christian history has repeated

Deuteronomy and Joshua—killing enemies, creating refugees, seizing land and resources, and exploiting others' labor. Today it is often done by international corporations, sometimes under state sanction. Although contemporary Christianity is repenting of some of its sins, it still has miles to go in fulfilling the purposes of God in salvation geography.

— 8 —

Modern Israel and the Land

OUR REVIEW of the biblical vision of salvation geography offers a much-needed perspective on the territorial impasse we see in the contemporary Israeli/Palestinian conflict.

Any assessment of the modern state of Israel must begin with respect for its appreciation of the land. But that assessment must also begin with a confession of Christianity's abysmal record in salvation geography. It is Christians who have committed some of the grossest violations of what Jesus taught in this regard, Christians who claim Jesus gives us the definitive reading of Israel's history, and Christians who should recognize that Jesus calls us to a new way to possess territory. With regard to the Jewish people especially, it is Christians who segregated Jews in ghettos in medieval Europe, engaged in pogroms in Eastern Europe, and perpetrated the Holocaust in Central Europe. It is Christians who dragged their feet in granting refuge to persecuted and beleaguered Jews in modern Europe. It is Christians and their failure to live salvation geography who created the conditions that produced modern Zionism.

In its emergence and development modern Zionism

copied the model of European nation-states, the very states that perpetrated the evils just mentioned, as reviews of the history of Zionism have repeatedly pointed out. In this respect the modern state of Israel is a rerun of 1 Samuel 8, a decision to be "like the nations" instead of a redeemed alternative to the nations. Theodore Herzl himself declared Zionism's aim to be the establishment of a state as Jewish as England was British, with the consequence that modern Israel has followed the sad example of European states in its methods of appropriating territory.[17] Moreover, since its establishment the state of Israel has found support for its policies in those militant chapters of its history when it first occupied the land under Joshua and then functioned for a few centuries as an independent nation-state. Israel does not seem to be looking for guidance from the much longer era of the Diaspora.

It is not necessary to detail here all of the unholy things that have been done in Israel/Palestine in the last one hundred years (to pick an arbitrary length of time)—how many Israelis or Palestinians have been killed, how many Palestinian villages have been erased from the map, how many refugees have been produced, how much property has been expropriated, how many suicide bombers have blown themselves and others up, and how many Palestinians have been reduced to virtual servitude or destitution. There are people who keep these scores. Atrocities have been and are continuing to be committed on both sides, and both sides are in need of the biblical message of salvation geography.

It is also not necessary to recite once more the justifications each side offers for its policies and actions: that it is justifiably responding to previous victimization, that it is merely exercising its rights, that it is merely retaliating for the other side's provocations. In defense of their expropriation of Palestinian property some Israelis explain that they cannot go back to Vienna and reclaim ancestral homes there which already long ago were appropriated by others. They too can say, like Palestinians I have personally heard, "That house over there is where I used to live. It was our home for generations."[18] However, pleading victimization at the hands of others—"they did it to us"—as an excuse for doing the same thing in turn is actually a self-indictment rather than an excuse. It is an admission that expropriating property and creating refugees are reprehensible deeds. It is not a license to repeat a crime just because one was committed against you. An outrage against atrocities that expresses itself in retaliation is not yet true outrage. True outrage recoils against retaliatory atrocities.

Special Dispensation for Israel?

The popular perception among many Christians seems to be that Israel's connection with their land is unique among peoples of the earth and not found anywhere else. Therefore many Christians today grant Israel a special dispensation to resort to measures in taking the land that might not be excused elsewhere. They would take the story of Israel's original conquest of the land as a divine concession to modern Israel to use the methods it does in retaking the land. They would excuse Israel from obedience to the call of Jesus toward a new policy with regard to the land, not recognizing that the teaching of Jesus with respect to the land only articulated with increased clarity and persistence the message the Jewish community already possessed in its prophets and reflected in Second Temple literature. The truth is, Israel is not granted a unique and special dispensation to resort once more to the Deuteronomy /Joshua pattern to reoccupy its land. Rather Israel is called still today to follow Abraham and be a model of a new way—God's way—to possess land. Modern Israel's record is not conducive to the fulfillment of the vision of Isaiah 2 and Micah 4, which see nations of the world coming up to Jerusalem to "learn war no more." Today Jerusalem happens to be a place to learn how to make war, and to make it very effectively!

Popular support in the western world for modern Israel, including that of many Christians, comes from the unquestioned assumption of the legitimacy of nationalisms established and maintained by military might. In the minds of most American Christians "national security" assured by military means remains an unquestioned dogma, a dogma applied by most American Christian apocalyptists to the land of Israel. Where violence, bloodshed, and war have not succeeded in establishing a divine rule of peace and love and righteousness—from King David through the Maccabees, to the Jewish revolt of 66-70 C.E. and the insurrection of Bar Kochba, to the crusades of 1095 and the New Jerusalem of Münster in 1535—many Christian believers still reassure themselves that this is the policy Jesus Christ will pursue at his second advent, and that when Christ does it, it will finally work. Behind this "hope" is the persistently cherished ideology that using violence to possess territory will work because God's way ultimately remains the way of violence.

Seeing the kingdom of God as ultimately imposed by force makes it not too different in the end from the kingdoms of the world it is supposed to replace. Yet this is the picture one gets from popular "prophetic" works such as Hal Lindsey's *Late Great Planet Earth* and the popular "Left Behind" series of Tim Lahaye and Jerry Jenkins. In these scenarios the future kingdom of God does not so much replace the violence of human history as provide the culmination of it. Christ's future millennial reign gets portrayed as a totalitarian rule to eclipse all totalitarianisms, although it is of course a benevolent totalitarianism and welcomed after the slaughter of Armageddon by most of what is left of the human race. The dispensationalist scheme of things admits that a large proportion of humanity left after Armageddon does not sincerely welcome the thousand-year reign of Christ but rebels when it gets a chance at the end of that reign, disclosing the fact that coercion did not achieve the genuine submission of people to the reign of Christ.

God has given us a different picture in Jesus of Nazareth. As already discussed in chapter five, Jesus showed God's way of possessing territory under the rule of God. And the second coming of Jesus Christ will be in character with the first. The second advent will see the appearance of "this same Jesus," not a different one, coming to complete the work of salvation initiated in the first advent, not to abandon or turn his back on the work of salvation initiated in the first advent.

We should address here an objection occasionally raised by defenders of Israel's policies: that Israel should not be held to a higher standard than that of other modern nations. Those who voice this objection must accept its implications, that as a nation Israel will reap the same consequences, the same fortunes and misfortunes, as have befallen all nation-states that have committed themselves to the way of violence. If Israel accepts this implication, then good luck! Nations rise and fall, and Assyria, Babylonia, and Persia—and Israel from David to the exile—are only beginning examples. Yet Israel wants to have it both ways: not to be held to a higher standard than other secular nations, and yet to be justified by a religious canon of scripture in its claim to establish a Jewish state in this particular land.

In the end, Israel cannot have it both ways. If it wants to be a *Jewish* state, it must be measured against the central insights of its Jewish heritage, its own prophetic tradition. There can be hardly any doubt that modern Israel's claim to the land rests upon the ancient biblical promise. Why otherwise would it claim this land? If that is so, Israel is obligated to sanctify the land in accordance with the conditions God attached to the promise. But if Israel asks to be measured by the standards of typical modern nation-states, it forfeits its right to special privilege and support. Holding Israel to a higher standard than that of other nations is actually a compliment, a recognition of Israel's higher calling, something not expected of other nations that do not possess Israel's ethical heritage.

Only Life in Israel Authentically Jewish?

Some zealous Israelis have encouraged immigration of (all?) Jews to Israel on the argument that only life in that state is authentically Jewish and offers Jews full freedom to observe all the laws of Torah. In the words of one rabbinic tradition, "It could be said of a Jew living among the *goyim* (Gentiles) that 'he is like one who has no God'" (b. Ket. 110b. In Prior, 203). That view makes all Jews living outside the land by definition not fully observant. In answer to this we can note that the majority of Jews in the land of Israel today are secular and not observant Jews. Moreover, it is not possible for all thirteen million-plus Jews in the world to live in the state of Israel, whose population is already over half the concentration of that of the Netherlands.

The argument that only life in the land can be authentically Jewish occasionally appeals to the Pentateuchal laws of agriculture, commandments concerning the fallowing of fields and first fruit offerings. It would seem that observance of these commandments depends upon engagement in agriculture itself, not whether agriculture is within some traditional boundaries. After all, the actual boundaries of biblical Israel varied over the centuries. It is possible today for conscientious Jews to observe the same laws anywhere in the world, given modern communication and travel. Indeed, it is not only possible but mandatory if God gave Abraham the world.

Actually, Jewish claims about not being able to observe certain laws outside the area from Dan to Beer Sheba, particularly laws related to agriculture, may have more to do with discriminatory restrictions against owning land historically placed upon Jews in Europe than it has to do with the intrinsic nature of Jewish laws about agriculture itself. What is needed for observance of Torah is not any special geographical location, but commitment to such observance and sufficient freedom of religion, including freedom of pilgrimage to Jerusalem. It is much easier for an American Jew to make pilgrimage to Jerusalem today than it was for a Galilean Jew at the time of Jesus.

Israel failed to observe important laws of Torah already when it existed as an independent nation and the inhabitants of the land could observe these laws. To make up for previously neglected Sabbaths, 2 Chronicles reports that the land should lie desolate for seventy years "to fulfill the word of the LORD by the mouth of Jeremiah" (2 Chron 36:21). John Howard Yoder in *The Politics of Jesus* notes that people at the time of Jesus ingeniously sidestepped the law of jubilee when they could and should have observed it (66ff.). Moreover, even though today the state of Israel has been established for nearly sixty years and seeks to be a Jewish state, it seems to be in no hurry to institute observance of the land's seventh year agricultural sabbath and jubilee laws enjoined in the Old

Testament. It is inconsistent for modern Israelis to argue that Jews should really live in the land to be authentically Jewish when Jews in the land may be less observant than those living outside it, even though one may see some devout Jews waving sheaves at the Western Wall during the Feast of Weeks. They may actually be pilgrims from New York.

The truth is, many Jews today prefer to live elsewhere than in Israel, many of them precisely because they believe the policies of the state of Israel are inconsistent with the truest character of Judaism and with God's intent for how Israel should possess the land. In that sense their view is the opposite of that mentioned above. They hold their Diaspora Judaism to be as authentic, if not more so, as the Judaism of the state of Israel. Says Jacob Neusner, a contemporary American Jew, "I maintain that there is an *Israel* in America. That is, a valid Jewish way of life, an authentic and enduring Judaic religious expression, a continuing Jewish social entity ('community,' or 'people,' or 'ethnic group'), do endure here." Neusner discusses the dilemma of Zionism and Judaism. Zionism has produced a secular state that includes Arab Muslim and Christian citizens, whereas Judaism is a faith that does not need a particular state. Furthermore, notes Neusner, "Until the present time, five times more Israelis have settled in America than American Jews in Israel" (Neusner, ix, 33).

It is only fair to add that many voices inside Israel and in America speak prophetic criticism of the policies of the Israeli government, as found in articles in the *Jerusalem Post* and even more in the periodical *Tikkun* and its Web site. And in this connection we could and should credit the contributions of Diaspora Jews for centuries to the cultures of the Western world despite the recurrent discrimination and persecutions and even pogroms they experienced. True, there have been less than desirable

Jewish models in the fields of entertainment and finance in modern America, but on balance the Jewish contribution in medicine, education, law, the sciences, philanthropy, humanities, art, and industry has been a sanctifying influence in Western society. Indeed, Jewish people might well qualify as exhibit A of creativity and constructiveness of a people made refugees and world citizens by the persecution inflicted upon them. To an amazing extent they have followed the counsel of Jeremiah, whether consciously or not, to seek the peace and welfare of the lands where they have come to live. Whether or not on Jeremiah's advice, and whether intended that way or not, their contributions should be considered a fulfillment of God's call to Abraham and his descendants to be a blessing to the world and of Israel to be a light to the nations. Jews sometimes downplay the contributions they have made to many cultures of the world because of fear of anti-Semitism.

The thesis of this book does not depend upon whether the Jewish people will confess Jesus of Nazareth as their messiah. The question that confronts us is whether we will *all* accept what God says to us in our respective Scriptures about possessing territory. For unless we find God's way of sanctifying the lands in which we live, those lands will continue to be polluted with bloodshed and will continue to vomit out their inhabitants, creating refugees whose displacement leads to population disturbances elsewhere, thereby perpetuating the problem with a domino effect throughout history.

In his mission, Jesus confronted his Jewish community with the persistent invitation to adopt a new mentality and a new policy concerning how to relate to the Gentile world in its possession of territory. In doing so Jesus and the apostolic community were reading their own Jewish canon of scripture.

A Defense of Palestinian Policies?

A critique of modern Israel should not be construed as a defense of Palestinian policies, for these are even more unapologetically predicated upon the use of force and violence to defend territory. It was conquest that first brought Jerusalem under Islamic rule in 638 C.E. That conquest was not a particularly violent or bloody one, because of Patriarch Sophronius's surrender of Jerusalem to the Caliph Omar. Had Jerusalem not surrendered, its resistance would no doubt have precipitated bloodshed.

The message of this book is most relevant to Islam's understanding of possessing territory, given its historic record on the sword and conquest. Historic Islam's ultimatum was "submission or the sword" (the word "Islam" means submission). But in view of Islam's rejection of the Jewish and Christian Scriptures as falsified or corrupted, the argument of this book to reject conquest and violence as a means to possess territory must be pursued with Muslims on other grounds. As mentioned in the introduction, this book is addressed to Christians. I would hesitate to appeal to Muslims to heed their authorities, the Qur'an and Hadith, on the subject of possession of land, as any Christian who has looked into these writings can understand. Islam has a long record of territorial conquest. But as victims of conquest and colonialism in modern history, Muslims may be invited to rethink their traditional views of possession of territory.

Defenders of Palestinian resistance to Israel's policies may claim that Palestinian Christians stand in solidarity with Muslims, indicating that their resistance is not a particularly Muslim thing. But the majority of Palestinian Christians have emigrated, leaving the conflict increasingly a Jewish-Islamic one. Where even in modern times Christians used to constitute 10 percent of the Palestinian population, they are now scarcely two percent of it. Defenders of Islam of course are quick to explain that the word Islam itself is related to the word peace (salaam). And selected verses of the Qur'an can be invoked to show that Islam teaches peace (see, for example, *The Christian Century*, March, 2001). In the end, however, the bottom line remains: unlike what we have in the Jewish-Christian tradition, there is in Islam no basic doctrine one can appeal to that the meek shall inherit the earth. But that doesn't preclude our offering Muslims the challenge of this teaching of Jesus and the Old Testament prophets, that God is seeking to coach the human race toward a new paradigm with respect to occupation of territory on God's earth.

The Bible's comprehensive teaching on how to possess territory is what, in the final analysis, must govern our reading of the Middle East problem. This is what is meant by salvation history and salvation geography. To accept the invitation to a new way of acquiring and possessing space is not without complications and problems, but the alternative is much worse. We can only leave to God the consequences of modern Israel's refusal to follow the way that has been articulated in the prophets and in Jesus. Whatever those consequences, they never cancel the standing invitation or preclude the possibility and privilege of returning to God's design for possessing territory.

In one of his recent books Bernard Lewis writes, "If the peoples of the Middle East continue on their present path, the suicide bomber may become a metaphor for the whole region, and there will be no escape from a downward spiral of hate and spite, rage and self-pity, poverty and oppression" (Lewis, 159). It is a frightening prospect. I fear that most suicide bombers, and even more those who recruit and send them on their mission, do not stop to think of what their policy does to their own society. However, suicides can also be the acts of nations, not just of individuals. Without planning it, Israel may be preparing itself to repeat history, committing national suicide as it did in the events leading to the exile in 587 B.C.E., in the Jewish war of 66-70 C.E., and in Bar Kochba's revolt of 135 C.E. And America's current policies may well consign us to eclipse, not only as a nation that proposes to be the "a city on a hill," but also as a world power.

The Holy Land will no doubt always remain the Holy Land insofar as it is the place of historic events of salvation history, even if, God forbid, it were to be reduced to a pile of radioactive rubble. But in recent times it has been tragically desecrated by the violence perpetrated in it and has not realized what God intended in the promise to Abraham. Political leaders, diplomats, and pundits offer proposals to reduce the violence and to chart a "roadmap" to peace. Most such proposals are couched within the framework of the usual assumptions of "peace with security," code language for continued dependence upon military power. Such searches for peace may be sincere and sometimes even desperate, but if the parties searching for such peace are not willing to change their perspective and look at a whole new approach, then an unending series of peace proposals will remain exactly that, unending. What we need is resolute commitment to salvation geography as a way of prevention, a refusal to go down the way of violence in the first place.

This encouragement to Christians not to endorse or justify Israeli policies today does not deny the right of Jewish people to live in their historic land. It questions only their methods. Most Christians do not, and I vehemently do not, endorse or justify Palestinian terrorism or suicide bombing. How could I in view of this entire book's argument that conquest and violence is not the way to come into possession of or even to defend territory?

The Way of Prevention

This book offers no quick fix for the Israeli/Palestinian problem. Too much popular thinking is governed by expectations of crisis intervention rather than prevention. Among schoolboys on the playground an insult can escalate to a shove, a shove to fists, fists to knives, knives to guns, and guns to death. Too often parties to a conflict look for help, if they look for help at all, when the conflict has reached its deadly stage, and the help they then look for is a magical rescue that does not require them to abandon the addiction to violence they chose at the outset and refuse to renounce. Happy are those who have the sanity to see the folly of the way of violence from the start and have committed themselves to strategies of peacemaking and reconciliation early in the game.

The ultimate purpose of this book is not to offer solutions that fail to re-examine the cause of the problems. The purpose of this book is to urge prevention, to point to another way of possessing territory. Moreover, the ultimate purpose is not to focus only upon the land in dispute in the Middle East but to widen our horizons to see that the new way of possessing territory that God invited Israel to model, beginning in its corner of the world, was intended to be a pattern for all peoples, including you and me, in the spot where we live.

A Christian view of Israel and its relationship to the holy land should not be guilty of supercessionism, that is, the view that Christianity supersedes or replaces Judaism and that therefore Judaism should really disappear, and with it any special attachment on their part to the historic land of Israel.[19] Paul argues in his letter to the Romans that God's promise to Abraham is never revoked, and therefore any descendants of Abraham, genetic or spiritual, are permitted to cherish the historic land of Israel, and even seek to dwell there, with two provisos: first, that they possess it the way Abraham did, and second, that they recognize that God's promise to Abraham extended to the whole earth, as the Jews themselves came to see already before the time of Jesus and Paul. Indeed, the global extension of the promise to Abraham in pre-Christian Judaism is most likely where Jesus and Paul got it. The problem of salvation geography is not the difficulty of the Jewish or Christian communities attempting to live salvation on a global scale. The problem is the impossibility of doing it on the geographically circumscribed scale of a nation-state.

— 9 —
The Implications of Holy Land

PARTIES TO the Middle East conflict have made the name of that land a touchy subject. Should it be called Palestine or Israel? In Hebrew scripture the land was first called Canaan and was known by only that name until well after the Hebrews had settled in it, and that name is remembered even as late as Psalm 135:11. It was called the land of Israel for the first time in 1 Samuel 13:19 and thereafter usually known by that name in Israel's Scriptures. The name Judah, originally the name of a son of Jacob and then the name of a leading tribe, became the name of the southern kingdom after the divided monarchy (ca. 820 B.C.E.).

The name Palestine comes from the term Philistine, which originally designated the people who migrated into the Gaza area of Canaan around 1190 B.C.E., sometime after the entry of the Hebrews into Canaan's hill country. Despite King David's decisive victories over the Philistines, they survived in several small city states but later disappeared as a distinct people in the Hellenization of the eastern Mediterranean world, followed by its Christianization and then Islamicization from 638 C.E. onward. The Romans named the southern portion of the province of Syria "Syria Palaestina," one administrative district of Syria. Next, Muslims similarly named it Felastin. In modern times the name Palestine was revived as an official title when the British were given a mandate for the government of the country in 1920.

More suggestive than any of the above terms is "holy land," a term found for the first time, and the only place in the Bible, in Zechariah 2:12: "The LORD will inherit Judah as his portion in the holy land, and will again choose Jerusalem." According to Robert Wilken, "Second Maccabees is the first Jewish writing to use the term *holy land* since the prophet Zechariah and the first in which the term occurs in Greek" (Wilken, 1992, 24-25). Philo of Alexandria uses the term frequently, although he chose not to live in the land. The term holy land occurs for the first time in Christian literature in Justin Martyr's *Dialogue with Trypho the Jew*, just after 135 C.E. (Wilken, 1992, 57).

"In the years after the war with the Romans in 70 C.E. the term 'holy land' was a kind of code word among Jews to express the messianic hope that the exiles would return to Israel and reestablish a Jewish kingdom. For this reason, Christians at first rejected the term" (Wilken, 1986, 679). In due course, rabbinic reflection constructed a scale of degrees of holiness for areas of the holy land itself. Jerusalem was more holy than the land in general, the temple area holier than the rest of Jerusalem, and the specific courts of the temple increasingly holy, culminating in the temple's holy of holies. Today some ultra-Orthodox Jews therefore would refuse to walk on the Temple Mount even if they could, lest they tread upon the historic sacred spot of the holy of holies.

So far as I have been able to discover, Jerusalem was called holy for the first time in Christian vocabulary by

Cyril of Jerusalem, bishop of that area beginning around 348 C.E. He did so likely because its sites had become centers of pilgrimage for Christians, especially after Constantine. As Bishop of Jerusalem during this period of the burgeoning pilgrimage movement, Cyril structured rites for pilgrims, such as those reported by the famous woman pilgrim Egeria. But according to Robert L. Wilken, "In all of Christian literature before the sixth century [the term holy land] occurs less than a dozen times, and usually as a phrase to reject. Only rarely did it refer to the present province of Palestine, and it had no religious significance for Christians" (Wilken, 1986, 679).

And yet any pilgrim or tourist who visits Israel today and travels the circuit of the chief holy places soon discovers that these and scores of other places in Israel have been centers of pilgrimage and of monastic life from as early as three hundred years after the time of Jesus. Today holy land has become a common term for the land of Israel/Palestine.

With the rise of Islam in the early 600s C.E. Muslims have joined the company of Jews and Christians in also calling Jerusalem al Quds, the holy. Muhammad at first directed prayers toward Jerusalem until the Jewish community around Medina refused to recognize him as a messenger of God, after which he redirected prayers toward Mecca. Muhammad is nevertheless supposed to have made his *miraj*, his night journey, or ascension to heaven, from Jerusalem (perhaps, as Zwi Werblowsky once quipped, because there were no direct flights from Mecca or Medina). Jerusalem's sanctity is what led to the building of the Dome of the Rock on what was at that time a deserted Temple Mount.

Holy People, Not Holy Rocks

Modern pilgrims to the Holy Land seem almost to believe its sanctity refers to something inherent in rocks and fields or in the structures upon them. But earth and water and the flora and fauna of this area do not recognize some artificial boundaries such as Dan or Beer Sheba where it might be thought holy land ends and unholy land begins. Nor does any spiritual meter ever register some charge of holiness on this side of the Jordan but not on the other. Land is not intrinsically holy within some arbitrarily defined borders, whether or not drawn according to biblical texts, only to become intrinsically unholy a few meters away. God doesn't grant some favorite country an inherent charge of holiness. Not even the sacred sites in salvation history can guarantee the holiness of the land. Such holiness "stem[s] ultimately from the special connection of Israel to God—and not from any particular property of 'holiness' inherent in that particular place" (Schechter, 274-75). "Its holiness, where expressed or implied, is not an inherent status, but totally dependent on God's decision to be present in [it] or [to] withdraw from it" (Janzen, 144). Its holiness is made a reality only as people sanctify the territory in which they dwell, the land where they sojourn with God.

It is imperative to note once more the distinction between land that may be called holy by virtue of events of salvation history and land that is holy by virtue of the quality of life of the people within it. Holy places may have lasting historical significance on some religious map. But holy land in the full sense is such only where people of faith live salvation geography by incarnating the message of salvation history.

Our review of the narrative of salvation history shows us that sanctification of the land—any land—embraces those values articulated already in Old Testament laws and prophets: respecting property rights; offering help to the poor and opposing the development of a society polarizing rich and poor; assuring justice in the courts; and respecting land as something not to be turned into a speculative commodity. This last value overlaps with many concerns of environmentalists today.[20] Sanctifying the land includes also those ethical principles articulated by Jesus in the Sermon on the Mount and in his entire public ministry, and by apostles in their New Testament epistles. Above all, sanctifying the land in which we live mandates the rejection of violence and bloodshed in all aspects of acquiring and stewarding space on God's green earth.

In the turbulent Sixties in America, when arson marked some urban riots, a colleague of mine was talking with his neighbor about what they would do if someone attempted to torch their houses. The neighbor said he would shoot such an arsonist. My colleague said he would not. Human life was more sacred than personal property. That attitude is just one of the marks of sanctification of one spot in the world.

If we should not regard the historic land of Israel as alone holy and the rest of the globe as unholy, neither should we expect any part of the planet to be either totally unholy or perfectly sanctified. Nevertheless, our commitment to consecrate our corner of the world counts even if our achievement is quite imperfect.

Holy Land and Refugees

One of the marks of holy land is its relevance for an acute problem that beset societies in ancient times and continues in the modern world, as reported periodically in the evening news. It is the perennial matter of refugees and illegal immigration. "Almost 35 million displaced people were living in refugee camps or other temporary shelters last year," reported the June 28, 2003, issue of the *Christian Century*.

In one respect the story of the Hebrews can already be told as the story of immigrants and refugees. Whatever else we may wish to say about Abraham and Sarah, they were definitely immigrants into the land of Canaan, and as we have seen, the land hospitably received them. The Hebrew tribes of the exodus were refugees from Egyptian slavery whom the land of Canaan did not want to receive. But they occupied it anyway and unfortunately created refugees in turn. Because their policies in the land over the next centuries defiled the land, according to the critique of their own prophets, they were themselves made refugees, this time by forced deportation.

In the deportation to Babylon the Jews succeeded better than they did in their own land in sanctifying that land and other lands to which they went, thus forwarding God's gracious purposes in salvation history and salvation geography. In the return of the exiles in response to the decree of Cyrus we see again an instance of immigration and, in the Roman empire's banishment of Jews from Judea after the Bar Kochba revolt, another chapter in the history of the Jews as refugees.

If the desecration of land produces refugees, the sanctification of land does the opposite. It attracts and welcomes refugees and creates a home for them. Considerable population movements may be precipitated by political or religious persecution and also by natural disasters. Sometimes they are caused by the lure of healthy religious, economic, and political social systems that attract people caught in a less happy society. Migration can thus have both a push and a pull. The push is usually obvious—civil strife and economic need. Refugee flight can become desperate when prompted by the threat of genocide, as was the case of the Hebrews seeking to escape Egypt. Or refugees from Cambodia under the Khmer Rouge. The lure should be equally obvious. It is often the attraction of a relatively "holier" land, the attraction of a country whose quality of social, political, and economic life promises peoples caught in conflict a stability, peace, security, freedom, and order they cannot find in their previous unhappy circumstances. The more holy a given land, the greater may therefore be its problem of refugees and immigrants knocking at its doors.

However, massive population relocations are not efficient and often not the happiest solution to the problems causing them. A relatively holier land should not therefore be expected to absorb a perpetual and unending stream of refugees or immigrants, perennially integrating populations produced by violent lands. For this reason people of a holy land, if it is truly holy, should seek to address the cause of refugees. However, the permanent solution to the social disorders that produce refugees is rarely if ever the external imposition of law and order, but rather the communication of those values that generate peace, goodwill, generosity, prosperity, and cooperation. Too often recently Americans have seen the solution to violent societies that produce refugees to be added violence by sending in the military.

Land that possesses the grace to accept immigrants and refugees incurs a risk and a task. The risk is that immigrants and refugees might bring with them too much of the unholy cultural baggage that made their society one they fled. The task is to help immigrants and refugees to become aware of what values shape the society they want to enter, and to help them adopt the best of those values.

There is yet another side to this phenomenon of

refugees and migrations. When people of faith, Jews or Christians, are themselves made refugees, as they not infrequently are because of discrimination against them, they have often contributed to the sanctification of the land to which they flee, precisely because every corner of the world is capable of being hallowed. According to the biblical narrative of salvation history Abraham is the first immigrant who does this in the land in which he settles down, as we have seen.

Holy land has to do with welcoming refugees and immigrants *and* trying to remove the causes and alleviate the problems of such population dislocations as much as possible. Where land is sanctified, it engenders contentment and stability and fosters love of home. But where unholy land produces refugees, sanctified land performs a redemptive function.

Pilgrim People on the Earth

This points up a fundamental privilege of all people who heed the call to sanctify the land in which they dwell. Since their God is the God of all the earth, they can be a pilgrim people and be at home with God wherever destiny calls them, and sanctify the land wherever they live. An illustration would be the experience of my own people, the Mennonites, who were persecuted or discriminated against in Europe for some time after their founding in the sixteenth century. They have moved from Switzerland to southern Germany and France, to Pennsylvania and many other parts of the United States and Canada. Other Mennonites have moved from the Netherlands to Prussia (now northern Poland) to Ukraine to the prairies of the United States and Canada, to the San Joaquin and Fraser Valleys, and even to places such as Paraguay and Belize. In Holmes County, Ohio, Amish people make up just over half of the population. The crime rate and proportion of people on welfare in that county is one of the lowest in Ohio. Although this is admittedly not the only index of sanctification of the land, it is surely a valid one. Where a crime such as drug use is discovered among the Amish, it is a singular enough event to make the national evening news.

There is a story of possession of land in one corner of our world that merits mention here. While far from a perfect example, it shows that territory can be settled peacefully by immigrants. The story is told in Calvin Redekop's *Strangers Become Neighbors* (1980). From 1926 to 1947 three successive groups of Mennonites settled in the "green hell" of the Paraguayan Chaco, so called because of its summer heat. First 1,778 Mennonites came there from Canada in 1926. Then 2,041 refugees from Communist Russia in 1930 and 1931. Finally 2,256 more Russian Mennonites who had escaped with the retreating German army in World War II became refugees in 1947 and 1948. They ended up in Paraguay because no other country would take them in.

The vast Chaco was home to several thousand migrant Indians, mainly of two tribes, perhaps subsisting there because they had been pushed into the jungle by the Paraguayan military. But the land proved able to sustain a much higher population, given modern agriculture and industry. The groups of Mennonite immigrants referred to above bought land and developed farms and cooperatives to process cotton, peanuts, dairy products and beef. From the outset they faced the challenge of relating to the local Indian population. Although three Mennonites lost their lives in contacts with the Indians, the settlers refused to retaliate or resort to violence. Instead, this immigrant community organized and developed a mission to the Indians, a program to employ Indians on Mennonite farms and industries, and also to settle Indians on farms themselves and offer them education and medical services. Much of this enterprise received economic support from Germany, the Netherlands, Canada and the United States, to be sure, but also required much local sacrifice on top of the pioneering struggles of the immigrants.

The end result is a successfully functioning community of European settlers and Native South Americans that has given the "green hell" of the Chaco economic prosperity and multi-ethnic coexistence. No one claims the area is a paradise, socially, economically, or religiously, and its residents admit that they face continuing problems, but they are committed to a style of life I call salvation geography.

Mennonites too identify holy places in their salvation history and make pilgrimages to them. But more important for them has been the conviction that wherever they go as refugees or migrant people, they are never beyond the care and keeping of the one God of all the earth, and never beyond the conviction that any spot on earth is territory awaiting sanctification.

Many years ago a Kurdish student at Goshen College, where I taught for 33 years, was trying to generate support on campus for the Kurdish cause. Valid as aspects of that cause may have been at that time and may still be today, I could not suppress reservations about the kind of support he sought. I was prompted to reflect on my own family history. "Muhammad," I told him (not his real name), "I cannot really get behind the Kurdish cause of struggle for turf because my grandfather was born in Poland, my father was born in Ukraine, my mother was born in South Dakota, I was born in Saskatchewan, and my children were born in Indiana. I am part of a refugee and pilgrim people of God in the earth, so that wherever we live, we are at home with God." Our mission, I should have added at the time, is to try to contribute to the sanctification of whatever place we live.

Conclusion:
Heeding the Biblical
Narrative

MY READING of the biblical narrative accords with what I understand to be one of the principles of canon criticism—reading the whole story of the Bible for the understanding of salvation history. In "Beyond Criticism: Learning to Read the Bible Again" (*Christian Century*, April 20, 2004) Ellen Davis and Richard Hayes attach a list of "Nine theses on interpreting scripture," of which I find the following one particularly relevant. "Faithful interpretation of scripture requires an engagement with the entire narrative: the New Testament cannot be rightly understood apart from the Old, nor can the Old be rightly understood apart from the New. The Bible must be read 'back to front'—that is, understanding the plot of the whole drama in light of its climax in the death and resurrection of Jesus Christ. . . . Yet the Bible must also be read 'front to back'—that is, understanding the climax of the drama, God's revelation in Christ, in light of the long history of God's self-revelation to Israel."

For Christians Jesus himself is the demonstration of this principle. He does not come forward with new ideas, out of "left field" so to speak, but continues a reading of the Law and Prophets begun already within the canon of his Jewish heritage. What's more, Jesus does not expect the process to cease with him. As he himself says, when the Spirit comes, it will guide his followers into all truth (John 16:13). Jesus confirms a trajectory that he himself expects will continue in the history of the movement he began, which is why we draw conclusions about race and gender and human rights and democratic process that very possibly move legitimately beyond where the church was at the time of the apostles.

In novels or movies or stage plays the fortunes of characters often show fluctuations and reverses, requiring us to ponder the whole drama before drawing our conclusions about the playwright's intention. So it is in the biblical drama. Take the stories of Joshua or of King David by themselves, and conquest looks like a resounding success. But if we honor the whole biblical narrative and keep reading, we see the consequences of these conquests. For Christians the story continues in Jesus of Nazareth and the apostolic Church, disclosing where God is leading the drama of salvation history and salvation geography. We must take into account where the whole story goes in our formulation of ethical choices, not just look at the success or failure of characters in one particular scene.

In one respect, however, the biblical drama is quite different than stage play or movie. When stage plays and movies come to an end (often not soon enough!) we go back to real life. But the biblical drama continues, *and we are in it*. It is our job to review the entire biblical drama up to the present and decide which way we should go. Our task is, as the apostle Paul says, to heed what was written for our instruction (Rom 15:4; 1 Cor 10:11). Some people cavalierly ignore the biblical story in its entirety. Others fixate upon only one scene, and so miss or misinterpret the rather obvious meaning of the narrative as a whole.

And so I accept the whole biblical narrative as my primary source of instruction for salvation geography. Reading that story in its entirety, from the Garden of Eden through the promise to Abraham and Sarah, through the experiences of Israel in the land and in exile, to Jesus's reiteration of the Psalm 37 declaration that the meek shall inherit the land, to Paul's claim that God promised Abraham and his descendants the cosmos, I find that God intends every person on earth to find a home where he/she may dwell in peace and security. To be Christian and to accept the New Testament part of the biblical story calls us to a different way of relating geographically to peoples of the world than seizing territory or exterminating Canaanites, although the New Testament really elaborates upon a new way presented already in the Old Testament prophets. That new way is to present the gospel to all peoples of the world and, whether they accept it or not, to live as salt and light, to live in the world as followers of the way of Jesus.

The burden of this book is not really that strange, since it is in line with the basic thrust of Jesus's teachings. If it sounds new and strange, that might be because we are just becoming aware of what may have been a blind spot in Christian theology. We have for a long time seen many of the implications of salvation history for other aspects of ethical life—family, education, medical care, and recently race relations—but seemingly not yet for possession of land. But then traditional values such as family life and medical care are too often themselves the casualties of war over territory. It is time to see the implication of salvation history for the most fundamental ethical issue of all, salvation geography.

Misplaced Idealism?

Many readers taking the time to pick up this book may say that its view of possessing territory is hopelessly idealistic and utopian and will never work. Worse, they will say, even trying to shape policies according to such a view is an invitation to enemies to walk all over us and dispossess us.

One answer to this objection is to learn from history that the violent acquisition and defense of territory is no surer guarantee that we will hold onto it, or hold onto our lives. Nor is there any guarantee that we will live in peace in the meantime. Humanity's record on this planet is one of bloodshed, displacement, conquest, and kaleidoscopic change in domination and ownership of territory, and that not chiefly in spite of but because of people's commitment to the traditional impulse to resort to violence in controlling turf. Instead of securing the possession of territory, war creates the problem of refugees who have lost their land, and that problem is then solved only where and when people of other territories are willing to absorb the displaced populations. We can claim, with strong historical evidence, that far from being utopian, the irenic way to possess territory proposed in this book is the only one that has really "worked."

A second answer to the charge that our proposal is idealistic is to plead guilty and admit it. Yes, this is idealistic, just as the Sermon on the Mount and the rest of the teachings of Jesus, and much other teaching in scripture, are idealistic. Jesus's instruction, it is sometimes said, is only for private life, not for public policy. Or his teaching is for another time, the future kingdom of God, not for today, according to popular dispensationalist doctrine. And yet this idealistic message of Jesus never ceases to haunt us, stir our consciences, and inspire our imagination. More than that, over the centuries of history this message of Jesus has produced countless organizations, institutions, and programs that perform acts of kindness, mercy, justice, forgiveness, and goodwill by feeding the hungry, healing the sick, sheltering the homeless, and harboring the refugee. Yes, and it has also afforded peace and security to countless communities committed to the renunciation of violence and all that goes with it: terrorism, assassinations, destruction of property, rape, and ethnic cleansing. There are many communities on our globe that are practically utopias, at least compared to violence-torn parts of the world, although we should call these peaceful communities by their right name, samples of the rule of God. These are communities in which the radical message of Jesus has taken hold of the minds and hearts of people firmly enough for them to inherit and sanctify the land.

Most Christians advocate high ideals when it comes to marriage, holding, for example, that married people should not commit adultery. We don't scoff at this ideal just because sociologists tell us that a deplorably high percentage of people in American society do commit adultery. We don't, I hope, tell our youth that marital fidelity is an unrealizable ideal. The officiating minister at a traditional wedding ritual still usually invites the bride and groom to vow fidelity. We would certainly fault any presiding clergy who would mutter something during the ceremony about fidelity as unrealistic in view of the statistics in our society. Such demoralizing "realism" would hardly help the institution of marriage. We keep aiming for an ideal even when we know that too many people will not reach it, because aiming for an ideal helps more people achieve a higher standard of ethics than if we predict failure instead. Predict and expect failure from the outset, and that is exactly what we will get. And failure is what we get when we begin by rejecting the biblical ideal of possessing territory

It is puzzling and even ironic that the idealistic teachings of Jesus have often been called "hard sayings," when Jesus himself says, "My yoke is easy, and my burden is light" (Matthew 11:30). The sayings can become hard, to be sure, when people seeking to practice them bump up against a society threatened by them. That was the experience of Jesus himself. And it was the experience of those who first ventured to call for an end to segregation in America. Some of them became martyrs to that cause. More usually it is the refusal to take the way of Jesus that leads to hard consequences, as people in Northern Ireland, Rwanda, and Kosovo know.

Misplaced Confidence in Violence

The world decorates its war heroes and erects monuments to them and boasts that it is they who keep us safe and who secure our peace. However, the real but unsung heroes are those who from the start are committed to living with their neighbors in peace, keeping conflict from erupting to begin with. It is they who, if differences arise, settle them amicably, whether over some back fence between residential lots or along the 49th parallel in North America, the longest undefended border in the world.

At the time of the Iran-U.S. hostage crisis a Muslim student invited to speak at Goshen College remarked how often, where a blundering U.S. State Department created ill will abroad, some lowly Christian relief or development worker on the ground was able to undo much of the damage and create goodwill in its place. The state department, he suggested, should be handed over to a Christian relief and development agency.

We should therefore all be tired of the fatuous argument that it is the militaries of the world that keep the peace and keep us all safe. Look at the many countries of the world drowning in weaponry—and violence—where people perish not for lack of weapons but for want of a vision for peace. It is not the people of the world who engage in conflicts that bring us peace, but rather the people who choose the way of peace from the outset who keep their communities from erupting into conflict and violence. We have too long tolerated the illusion that it is war that gives us peace, when too often that kind of peace is only the bankruptcy and exhaustion of parties to the conflict.

A final word to those otherworldly people who would entertain the view that the mission of Jesus Christ and the rise of Christianity excuses us from concern for geography. To quote biblical scholar Waldemar Janzen, "The New Testament... does not abandon the concreteness of sacred Old Testament geography towards inwardness or other-worldliness, but towards a *new* theological significance of new (or old) places, a new significance which emerges from *new* acts of God in history." According to John's Gospel Jesus says the time will come when people will worship God neither in Jerusalem nor on Mt. Gerizim. But "these words do not take faith off the map; they redeem it from static attachment to certain holy places alone, so that the whole map can now become potential territory for God's election towards his ends" ("Geography of Faith: A Christian Perspective on the Meaning of Places," *Studies in Religion*, 1973).

Continued violence in struggles for control of territory in many parts of the world today demonstrates the perennial pertinence of the subject of salvation geography. Calling humanity to a new way of possessing land is the very first theme in salvation history, in the promise to Abraham. All that follows in the biblical narrative, supremely the life and message of Jesus, does not take salvation off the map. "Jesus and the early church, far from being aterritorial in theology, believed and lived out a new theologico-geographical realism," a new "geography of faith" (Janzen, 152).

To believe in Jesus Christ carries quite concrete implications for economics, ecology, sharing, concern for the poor, generosity toward the alien, resisting greed. To believe in Jesus sends us back to our geographical tasks with new grace and refined insight, equipped with the standards Jesus himself showed us in the words and deeds of his public ministry and in his passion. In the present hour it is our privilege as Christians to cherish any and all places of salvation history, from Jerusalem to those spots made sacred in church history and in our personal pilgrimage. And it is our privilege also to sanctify the areas in which we live, to steward them as gifts of God and to live in righteousness and peace with our neighbors.

Notes

1. http://www.geocities.com/Vienna/6640/zion/jewishproblem2.html

2. I am aware of the debate among biblical scholars over the historicity of the narratives of Israel's origins. See "History or Legend? Digging into Israel's Origins," by J. Maxwell Miller, *The Christian Century*, February 24, 2004. That debate does not alter the status of the biblical narratives as canonical literature accepted for ethical guidance in the Jewish community and in the Christian church.

3. Bernard W. Anderson, *Understanding the Old Testament,* (4th Edition, 1986), pp. 373-79. See also Deuteronomy in *The Interpreter's Dictionary of the Bible.*

4. According to the late Jonathan Sacks, chief rabbi of Great Britain, the Hebrew Bible contains only one commandment to love the neighbor but no less than thirty-six to love the stranger (*Christian Century*, September 20, 2005, p. 37).

5. I am indebted to Michael Prior in *The Bible and Colonialism* (1997) and personal conversations at Tantur in 1996 for drawing my attention to the number and force of these texts and their incompatibility with all modern Christian and even secular notions of morality, even in so-called just wars.

6. Perry Yoder, lecture at College Mennonite Church, January 2004.

7. Lectures at the Associated Mennonite Biblical Seminaries, October 28, 1983.

8. Brueggemann, 2nd edition, p. xiv. As shown by statements such as Judges 1:19, "they had chariots of iron," and Judges 3:2, "that [the] Israelites might know war," the author is explaining the situation of a bygone era, in the light of which commands in Deuteronomy 7:2 and 20:17, "you must utterly destroy them," are shown to be retrospective and to come from a much later era. In *A Light Unto My Path*, ed. Howard N. Bream, et al (1974), 500.

9. It was my privilege to hear Frankl lecture during my theological education at Garrett Seminary when I was there between 1955 and 1961.

10. Boundaries of the right kind are not inherently evil. They can be most useful for the administration of justice, healthcare, agriculture, education, and the maintenance of roads, railways, airports, and communication. Such boundaries may in fact be needed for linguistic, ethnic, geographical, and cultural reasons. But such boundaries should be subject to negotiation and change according to changing historical needs and circumstances.

11. Americans might remember the blow the Revolutionary war gave to Anglicanism on these shores. The Church of England was not particularly popular in this newly independent country and survived in America only by renaming itself the Episcopal Church and by showing itself sufficiently independent of English state control.

12. The International Christian Embassy is a conservative, mostly American, organization founded in 1980. It offers uncritical support for the modern state of Israel.

13. I am indebted to John E. Toews for drawing my attention to these texts in Second Temple Jewish literature.

14. So said Lou Silberman, Hillel Professor of Jewish Literature and Thought, Vanderbilt University, Nashville, Tennessee, at an Institute on Judaism I was privileged to attend there in the summer of 1971.

15. According to Wilken Jerusalem attracted so much pilgrimage that some early Muslim conquerors of the city thought Christianity also had a "law" requiring pilgrimage, as Islam had regarding Mecca.

16. Find a report on the web about either or both of these Moravian Indian towns, using a search engine such as Google.

17. Which is why Michael Prior calls the policy of the state of Israel colonialism. *The Bible and Colonialism: A Moral Critique.*

18. My wife and I heard such statements in the four months we spent in 1996 at Tantur, the Ecumenical Center for Theological Study just north of Bethlehem.

19. For more on a non-supercessionist view of Judaism that Christians can be invited to hold see John Howard Yoder's *The Jewish-Christian Schism Revisited*, edited by Michael G. Cartwright and Peter Ochs, 2003.

20. I am not unaware of the validity and importance of the concern of many Christians today for the ecological crisis and for the responsibility of Christians to address it. The focus upon salvation geography in this book does not ignore the legitimate concerns of ecology. Protecting the environment is indeed a legitimate part of sanctifying the lands in which we live. However, ecology has many spokespersons who can present its cause better than I can. Unfortunately it is often territorial conflicts that leave ecological disaster in their wake.

Bibliography

Anderson, Bernard W.
1986 *Understanding the Old Testament*, 4th Edition. Englewood Cliffs, N.J.: Prentice-Hall.

Brenneman, James E.
2004 *On Jordan's Stormy Banks: Lessons from the Book of Deuteronomy*. Scottdale, Pa.: Herald Press.

Brueggemann, Walter
1977 *The Land: Place as Gift, Promise, and Challenge in Biblical Faith*. Philadelphia: Fortress Press.

Burge, Gary M.
1993 *Who Are God's People in the Middle East?* Grand Rapids, Mich.: Zondervan Pub. House.

Carroll, James
2001 *Constantine's Sword: The Church and the Jews*. Boston: Houghton Mifflin.

Charles, R. H.
1985 *Apocrypha and Pseudepigrapha of the Old Testament*. Oxford: Clarendon Press.

Davies, W. D.
The Gospel and the Land: Early Christianity and Jewish Territorial Doctrine. Berkeley: University of California Press.

Gottwald, Norman
1979 *The Tribes of Yahweh: A Sociology of the Religion of Liberated Israel, 1250-1050 BCE*. Maryknoll, N.Y.: Orbis Books.

Habel, Norman C.
1995 *The Land is Mine: Six Biblical Land Ideologies*. Minneapolis: Fortress Press.

Janzen, Waldemar
1973 "Geography of Faith: A Christian Perspective on the Meaning of Places," In *Studies in Religion*.
1992 "Land." In *Anchor Bible Dictionary*, New York: Doubleday.

Jeremias, Joachim
  1958 *Jesus' Promise to the Nations*. Philadelphia, Pa.: Fortress Press.
Johnson, Philip, and Walker, Peter, eds.
  2000 *The Land of Promise: Biblical, Theological, and Contemporary Perspectives*. Downers Grove, Ill.: InterVarsity Press.
Kolleck, Teddy and Pearlman, Moshe
  1970 *Pilgrims to the Holy Land: The Story of Pilgrimage through the Ages*. New York: Harper and Row.
La Guardia, Anton
  2003 *War Without End: Israelis, Palestinians, and the Struggle for a Promised Land*. New York: St. Martin's Griffin.
Lewis, Bernard
  2002 *Want Went Wrong? Western Impact and Middle Eastern Response*. New York: Oxford University Press.
March, W. Eugene
  1994 *Israel and the Politics of Land: A Theological Case Study*. Louisville, Ky.: Westminster/John Knox Press.
Martens, Elmer A.
  1994 *God's Design: A Focus on Old Testament Theology*. Grand Rapids, Mich.: Baker Books.
May, Roy H., Jr.
  1997 *Joshua and the Promised Land*. New York: General Board of Global Ministries, United Methodist Church.
Miller, J. Maxwell
  2004 "History or legend? Digging into Israel's origins," In *The Christian Century*, February 24.
Neusner, Jacob
  1985 *Israel in America: A Too-Comfortable Exile?* Boston: Beacon Press.
Prior, Michael
  1997 *The Bible and Colonialism: A Moral Critique*. Sheffield, UK: Sheffield University Press.
Schechter, Jack
  1981 "The Theology of the Land in Deuteronomy," PhD dissertation, University of Pittsburgh.
Toews, John E.
  2004 *Romans: Believers Church Bible Commentary*. Scottdale, Pa.: Herald Press.

Wilken, Robert L.
1986 "From Time Immemorial? Dwellers in the Holy Land," In *The Christian Century*, July 30–August 6.
1992 *The Land Called Holy*. New Haven: Yale University Press.
Wright, N. T.
Jesus and the Victory of God, vol. 2. Minneapolis, Minn.: Fortress Press.
Yoder, John Howard
1997 *For the Nations: Essays Evangelical and Public*. Grand Rapids, Mich.: W. B. Eerdmans.
2003 *The Jewish-Christian Schism Revisited*, ed. Michael G. Cartwright and Peter Ochs. Grand Rapids, Mich.: W. B. Eerdmans.

Scripture, Apocryphal, and Pseudepigraphal Texts Index

Author Index

Subject Index

About the Author

Marlin Jeschke is Professor Emeritus of Philosophy and Religion at Goshen College in Goshen, Indiana, where he taught from 1961 to 1994. He received his BA from Tabor College, his Divinity degree from Garrett Theological Seminary (now Garrett-Evangelical), and his PhD from Northwestern University in Evanston, Illinois. He has been a postdoctoral visiting scholar at Harvard Divinity School and at Fuller Theological Seminary. In 1996 he and his wife Elizabeth spent four months at Tantur, the Ecumenical Center for Theological Study in Jerusalem. He is currently President of the Mennonite Historical Society in Goshen and a member of College Mennonite Church